EDITOR: Maryanne Blacker
FOOD EDITOR: Pamela Clark
DESIGN DIRECTOR: Neil Carlyle

• • •

DESIGNER: Lisa Rowell
SUB-EDITOR: Mary-Anne Danaher

• • •

ASSISTANT FOOD EDITOR:
Jan Castorina

ASSOCIATE FOOD EDITOR:
Enid Morrison

CHIEF HOME ECONOMIST:
Karen Green

HOME ECONOMISTS: Jon Allen, Jane Ash, Tikki Durrant, Sue Hipwell, Karen Hughes, Karen Maughan, Voula Mantzouridius, Alexandra McGowan, Louise Patniotis, Tania Thompson, Belinda Warn, Kathy Wharton

SEAFOOD CONSULTANT: Anna Phillips

STYLISTS: Carolyn Fienberg, Michele Gorry, Jacqui Hing, Rosemary De Santis, Vicki Liley, Anna Phillips, Belinda Warn

PHOTOGRAPHERS: Kevin Brown, Robert Clark, Paul Clarke, Justine Kerrigan, Ashley Mackevicius, Andre Martin, Robert Taylor

EDITORIAL ASSISTANT: Elizabeth Gray,

KITCHEN ASSISTANT: Amy Wong

• • •

HOME LIBRARY STAFF:

ART DIRECTOR: Robbylee Phelan

ASSISTANT EDITOR: Judy Newman

SECRETARY: Wendy Moore

• • •

EDITOR-IN-CHIEF: Sandra Funnel

PUBLISHER: Richard Walsh

• • •

Produced by The Australian Women's Weekly Home Library Division
Typeset by Photoset Computer Service Pty Ltd, and Letter Perfect, Sydney.
Printed by Dai Nippon Co Ltd, Tokyo, Japan
Published by Australian Consolidated Press, 54 Park Street Sydney
Distributed by Network Distribution Company, 54 Park Street Sydney
Distributed in the U.K. by Australian Consolidated Press (UK) Ltd (0604) 760 456. Distributed in New Zealand by Gordon and Gotch (NZ) Ltd (09) 654 397. Distributed in Canada by Whitecap Books Ltd (604) 980 9852. Distributed in South Africa by Intermag (011) 493 3200.

• • •

© A C P 1990 (Reprint)
This publication is copright. No part of it may be reproduced or transmitted in any form without the written permission of the publishers.

• • •

FRONT COVER: Clockwise from left: Seafood in Rich Tomato Sauce, page 65; Peppered Garlic Prawns, page 27; Steamed Whole Fish with Ginger Sauce, page 35. Enamel ware: Country Trader; napkin & board: Appley Hoare Antiques; table: Country Form. BACK COVER: Pork and Prawn Paupiettes with Blue Cheese Sauce, page 43. INSIDE FRONT COVER: Fish and Potato Scallops with Tartare Sauce, page 68

THE BEST SEAFOOD RECIPES

You can enjoy a delicious bonus with every bite of seafood; it not only tastes good, but is great for your health, too. Our recipes offer many fresh pleasures for you, and the kids can crunch and munch happily through a section just for them. First, though, read why top nutritionist Rosemary Stanton rates seafood so highly, then pick up tips on seafood preparation and making stock, all in our special guide and glossary at the back of the book

Pamela Clark
FOOD EDITOR

2 SOUPS	116 THE FACTS: BUYING, FREEZING AND STORING
8 ENTREES	118 SEAFOOD PREPARATION
28 SPECIAL OCCASION DISHES	121 YOUR GUIDE TO SEAFOOD
44 FAMILY MAIN MEALS	126 GLOSSARY
70 SNACKS AND LUNCHES	127 INDEX
100 FOR THE BARBECUE	
110 JUST FOR KIDS	

NOTE: *UK & USA conversion charts for cup and spoon measurements and oven temperatures are on page 117*

SOUPS

This section represents an international look at soups. We have used some wonderful fresh herbs to complement seafood and many tantalising oriental ingredients. Some recipes are suitable for family meals; others are perfect for entertaining. If you want to make your own fish stock, check the glossary or use vegetable or chicken stock cubes, as you prefer. Remember, these are salty.

SEAFOOD WITH COCONUT CREAM SOUP

We used ocean perch and green-lipped mussels in this soup; it is at its best served immediately it is made. This recipe is not suitable to freeze or microwave.

1 large potato, chopped
2 bacon rashers, chopped
1 large onion, chopped
210g can red salmon, drained
2½ cups fish stock
¼ cup sweet sherry
2 teaspoons tomato paste
½ cup dry white wine
2 tablespoons sour cream
150g can coconut cream
2½ cups milk
6 scallops
200g white fish fillets, chopped
6 mussels
6 uncooked prawns, shelled

Boil, steam or microwave potato until tender. Blend potato, bacon, onion and salmon until smooth. Combine stock, sherry, tomato paste and wine in large saucepan, bring to boil, stir in potato mixture, sour cream, coconut cream and milk. Return to boil, reduce heat, cover, simmer 15 minutes. Add seafood, heat without boiling until seafood is cooked.

Serves 8.

CREAMY LEEK AND OYSTER SOUP

Soup is best served immediately it is made. Bottled oysters can be used in this recipe; rinse under cold water before using. This recipe is not suitable to freeze.

60g butter
1 small leek, sliced
2 tablespoons plain flour
2 cups milk
2 cups water
½ large vegetable stock cube, crumbled
1 egg yolk
½ cup cream
24 oysters
few drops tabasco sauce
1 teaspoon light soy sauce

Melt butter in large saucepan, add leek, cook, stirring, for about 5 minutes (or microwave on HIGH for about 3 minutes) or until leek is soft. Add flour, stir constantly over heat for 1 minute (or microwave on HIGH for about 1 minute). Gradually stir in milk, water and stock cube, stir constantly over high heat (or microwave on HIGH for about 15 minutes) until mixture boils and thickens. Stir in combined egg yolk and cream, then oysters and sauces. Reheat without boiling.

Serves 4.

LEFT: Clear Soup with Garfish Twists.
RIGHT: From top: Creamy Leek and Oyster Soup; Seafood with Coconut Cream Soup.

Bowl & chest: The Country Trader

CLEAR SOUP WITH GARFISH TWISTS

Prepare soup as close to serving time as possible. Stock can be frozen for 3 months.

- 8 medium garfish
- 3 cups water
- 1 medium carrot, chopped
- 1 medium onion, chopped
- 1 stick celery, chopped
- 6 fresh parsley stems
- 6 black peppercorns
- 1 cup water, approximately, extra
- 1 small red pepper
- 16 snow peas
- 1 teaspoon light soy sauce
- 1 tablespoon chopped fresh ginger

Fillet 4 fish, reserve bones; cut each fillet into 2 strips. Twist 2 strips together, secure ends with toothpicks, cover, refrigerate.

Remove heads and clean remaining fish. Place cleaned fish and reserved bones from filleted fish into medium saucepan with the 3 cups water, carrot, onion, celery, parsley and peppercorns. Bring to boil, reduce heat, simmer 20 minutes (or microwave on MEDIUM HIGH for about 15 minutes). Strain through a fine sieve.

Add enough extra water to make 3 cups of stock. Cut pepper into strips.

Place stock into medium saucepan, bring to boil, add snow peas, pepper, fish twists and soy sauce. Cook over low heat for about 2 minutes (or microwave on MEDIUM HIGH for about 5 minutes) or until fish twists are cooked. Remove toothpicks, place fish into serving dishes, add stock, sprinkle with ginger.

Serves 4.

COCONUT CREAM SOUP WITH SPINACH AND KUMARA

We used ling fillets in this recipe. You can substitute 4 leaves silverbeet for ½ bunch English spinach, if desired. Soup can be made several hours ahead; keep, covered, in refrigerator. This recipe is not suitable to freeze.

- 15g butter
- 1 medium onion, finely chopped
- 1 medium kumara, chopped
- ½ teaspoon grated fresh ginger
- ½ teaspoon ground coriander
- 1 small fresh red chilli, finely chopped
- 2 cups fish stock
- 400ml can coconut cream
- 200g white fish fillets, chopped
- ½ bunch English spinach (20 leaves), chopped
- 1 teaspoon sugar

Heat butter in large saucepan, add onion, stir constantly over medium heat (or microwave on HIGH for 3 minutes) or until onion is soft. Add kumara, ginger, coriander and chilli, stir over heat further minute (or microwave on HIGH for 2 minutes).

Stir in stock and coconut cream, bring to boil, reduce heat, simmer, covered, for 15 minutes (or microwave on HIGH for about 10 minutes).

Add fish, spinach and sugar, simmer, uncovered, for about 10 minutes (or microwave, covered, on HIGH for about 5 minutes) or until fish is tender.

Serves 4.

CURRIED SMOKED FISH AND PEA SOUP

We used haddock in this recipe. Soup can be made up to a day ahead; keep, covered, in refrigerator. It can be frozen for up to 2 months. This recipe is not suitable to microwave.

- 30g butter
- 1 medium onion, finely chopped
- 2 sticks celery, chopped
- 2 medium potatoes, chopped
- 1 medium carrot, chopped
- 1½ tablespoons curry powder
- 5 cups (1¼ litres) water
- 1 cup milk
- 1 cup yellow split peas
- 500g smoked fish, chopped
- 2 tablespoons chopped fresh parsley
- 1 tablespoon lemon juice
- 1 teaspoon sugar

Heat butter in large saucepan, add onion, stir constantly over medium heat until onion is soft. Add celery, potatoes, carrot and curry powder, stir constantly over heat further minute. Add water, milk and peas, bring to boil, reduce heat, cover, simmer for about 1 hour or until peas are soft. Add fish, parsley, lemon juice and sugar, simmer, uncovered, further 2 minutes.

Serves 4.

BELOW: Left: Coconut Cream Soup with Spinach and Kumara; right: Curried Smoked Fish and Pea Soup. FAR RIGHT: Left: Crab and Watercress Soup; right: Prawn Bisque.

PRAWN BISQUE

Stock for soup can be made up to 4 days ahead; keep, covered, in refrigerator or freeze, without cream, for 3 months. This recipe is not suitable to microwave.

500g uncooked prawns
1 tablespoon oil
1 medium onion, chopped
1 stick celery, chopped
1 medium carrot, chopped
6 fresh parsley stems
2 bay leaves
½ teaspoon dried thyme leaves
10 black peppercorns, crushed
2 tablespoons tomato paste
½ cup plain flour
½ cup dry white wine
10 cups (2½ litres) water
½ large vegetable stock cube, crumbled
⅓ cup cream

Shell prawns, reserve shells. Heat oil in large saucepan, add reserved shells, onion, celery and carrot, stir constantly over high heat for about 5 minutes or until shells and vegetables are lightly browned. Add parsley, bay leaves, thyme, peppercorns, tomato paste and flour, stir constantly over heat until well combined.

Gradually stir in wine, water and stock cube, stir constantly over high heat until mixture boils and thickens slightly. Reduce heat, simmer, uncovered, for 30 minutes, stirring occasionally. Remove any scum that appears on top of soup during cooking. Strain soup through fine sieve, add cream, reheat soup gently without boiling.

Poach prawns in frying pan of simmering water for a few minutes or until cooked; drain, chop roughly. Serve with soup.

Serves 6.

Bowls, platter, napkin ring: Made Where

CRAB AND WATERCRESS SOUP

Prepare soup just before serving. This recipe is not suitable to freeze or microwave.

2 medium uncooked blue swimmer crabs
2 teaspoons butter
1 small carrot, chopped
1 stick celery, chopped
6 cups (1½ litres) water
30g butter, extra
1 small onion, chopped
1 small carrot, chopped, extra
¼ cup plain flour
1 cup chopped fresh watercress
¼ cup dry white wine
¼ cup cream

Remove flesh from body and claws of crabs. Melt butter in large saucepan, add crab shells, carrot and celery, stir constantly over medium heat for 5 minutes. Add water, bring to boil, reduce heat, simmer, uncovered, for about 30 minutes or until liquid is reduced by half.

Strain stock, discard shells and vegetables; reserve stock. You need 3 cups stock for this recipe. If you have evaporated too much liquid, make up to required amount with water.

Heat extra butter in large saucepan, add onion and extra carrot. Stir constantly over medium heat for about 5 minutes or until carrot is soft. Add flour, stir until smooth, stir constantly over low heat for 2 minutes. Gradually stir in reserved 3 cups stock, stir constantly over high heat until mixture boils and thickens.

Add watercress and crab, simmer, uncovered, for about 5 minutes or until crab is cooked. Blend or process mixture in several batches until smooth. Return soup to pan, add wine and cream, reheat without boiling.

Serves 4.

PRAWN WONTON SOUP

Soup is best prepared just before serving. Wontons can be made up to a day ahead; keep, covered, in the refrigerator or freeze for up to a month.

WONTONS
250g uncooked prawns
2 Chinese dried mushrooms
5 canned water chestnuts
2 green shallots, chopped
1 clove garlic, chopped
1 tablespoon oyster sauce
2 teaspoons light soy sauce
½ teaspoon sesame oil
1 teaspoon grated fresh ginger
1 teaspoon chopped fresh coriander
1 small carrot, finely grated
24 wonton wrappers
2 teaspoons cornflour
2 tablespoons water
1 medium red pepper, chopped
1 stick celery, chopped

STOCK
1 stick celery, chopped
1 medium onion, chopped
1 teaspoon black peppercorns
5 cups (1¼ litres) water
1 tablespoon oyster sauce
1 teaspoon sesame oil

BELOW: Clockwise from left: Prawn Wonton Soup; Clear Baby Octopus Soup; Tomato Soup with Chunky Seafood.

Wontons: Shell and devein prawns; reserve shells for stock. Soak mushrooms in enough boiling water to cover well for about 20 minutes or until soft, drain; discard stems.

Blend or process prawns, mushrooms, water chestnuts, shallots, garlic, sauces, oil, ginger and coriander until combined but not smooth. Transfer the mixture to a medium bowl.

Squeeze excess liquid from carrot (use your hand to do this); add carrot to prawn mixture, mix well.

Top each wrapper with a heaped teaspoon of prawn mixture, brush edge of each wrapper with blended cornflour and water. Fold wrappers diagonally in half, join opposite corners with the cornflour mixture.

Drop wontons into saucepan of boiling water, boil until wontons float to the surface; drain. Add wontons to pan of prepared stock, bring to boil, add pepper and celery, reduce heat, simmer, uncovered, for 3 minutes.

Stock: Combine prawn shells (not heads) with remaining ingredients in large saucepan, bring to boil, reduce heat, simmer, uncovered, for 20 minutes (or microwave on HIGH for about 15 minutes); strain, return to saucepan.

Serves 4.

CLEAR BABY OCTOPUS SOUP

Prepare soup just before serving. This recipe is not suitable to freeze or microwave.

500g baby octopus
4 cups (1 litre) water
2 small chicken stock cubes, crumbled
1 stick celery, chopped
3 teaspoons tom yum
1 teaspoon grated lime rind
2 tablespoons oyster sauce
1 tablespoon chopped fresh mint
2 teaspoons chopped fresh coriander
1 tablespoon chopped fresh basil
1 medium red pepper, chopped
4 green shallots, chopped

Discard head and beak from each octopus. Cut octopus through tentacles into 4 pieces. Combine water, stock cubes, celery, tom yum, rind and sauce in large saucepan. Bring to boil, add octopus, herbs and pepper, reduce heat, simmer, uncovered, for about 3 minutes or until tender. Sprinkle with shallots.

Serves 4.

TOMATO SOUP WITH CHUNKY SEAFOOD

We used ling fillets in this recipe. Prepare soup just before serving. Recipe unsuitable to freeze or microwave.

30g butter
1 medium red pepper, chopped
1 medium onion, chopped
1 medium leek, chopped
2 × 410g cans tomatoes
8 cups (2 litres) fish stock
1 tablespoon chopped fresh basil
tiny pinch ground saffron
3 tablespoons tomato paste
1 medium uncooked blue swimmer crab
250g uncooked medium prawns
375g thick white fish fillets, sliced
2 cloves garlic, finely chopped
1 tablespoon chopped fresh basil, extra

Heat butter in large saucepan, add pepper, onion and leek, stir constantly over low heat for about 10 minutes or until leek is tender. Add undrained crushed tomatoes, stock, basil, saffron and tomato paste, bring to boil, reduce heat, simmer, uncovered, for about 1 hour or until liquid is reduced by half.

Remove flesh from crab. Shell and devein prawns, leaving tails intact. Strain stock through fine sieve, discard vegetables, return stock to pan. Cover, bring to boil, reduce heat, add seafood. Simmer for about 3 minutes or until tender. Serve sprinkled with combined garlic and extra basil.

Serves 4.

ABOVE: Left: Cream of Mussel Soup; right: Fishyssoise Soup.

CREAM OF MUSSEL SOUP

Soup can be prepared several hours in advance; keep, covered, in refrigerator. Add cream, dill and mussels when reheating. Recipe unsuitable to freeze.

**1kg mussels
1 cup dry white wine
60g butter
8 green shallots, chopped
½ teaspoon curry powder
¼ cup plain flour
3 cups water
1 tablespoon tomato paste
1 large vegetable stock cube, crumbled
¾ cup cream
1 tablespoon chopped fresh dill**

Combine mussels and wine in large saucepan, bring to boil, cover, simmer for 3 minutes, remove mussels as they open (or microwave, covered, on HIGH for about 2 minutes). Strain cooking liquid and reserve.

Melt butter in large saucepan, add shallots and curry powder, cook for 2 minutes (or microwave on HIGH for about 2 minutes) or until shallots are soft. Stir in flour, stir constantly over medium heat for 2 minutes (or microwave on HIGH for about 1 minute). Remove from heat, gradually, add reserved liquid, water, tomato paste and stock cube. Return to heat, stir constantly over high heat (or microwave, uncovered, on HIGH for about 13 minutes, stirring occasionally) until mixture boils and thickens. Add cream, dill and mussels, heat without boiling.

Serves 4.

FISHYSSOISE SOUP

We used ocean perch in this recipe. Soup can be made up to 3 days ahead; keep, covered, in refrigerator. This recipe is not suitable to freeze.

**1 small leek, roughly chopped
4 medium potatoes, roughly chopped
250g white fish fillets, chopped
5 cups (1¼ litres) fish stock
⅓ cup cream
1 tablespoon chopped fresh chives**

Combine leek, potatoes, fish and stock in large saucepan, bring to boil, reduce heat, simmer for about 20 minutes (or microwave on HIGH for about 20 minutes) or until potatoes are soft. Blend or process soup in several batches until smooth, add cream and chives, reheat without boiling.

Serves 4.

ENTREES

Entrées are a wonderful way to explore flavours in small quantities, particularly with seafood you may never have tasted before. You can serve just one entrée as the smart start to a luncheon or dinner party, or make several for a dinner or a special barbecue. Our delicious and innovative seafood entrées can also be adapted to serve as main courses simply by increasing quantities to suit your diners.

BALMAIN BUG COCKTAILS

Cocktails, without sauce, can be prepared up to 2 hours ahead; sauce can be prepared several hours ahead. Keep both, covered, in refrigerator. This recipe is not suitable to freeze.

8 cooked Balmain bugs
1 cup shredded lettuce
1 small red Spanish onion, sliced
1 long thin green cucumber, thinly sliced
1 small red apple, sliced
1 tablespoon lemon juice
COCKTAIL SAUCE
2 tablespoons mayonnaise
1 tablespoon cream
1 tablespoon tomato sauce
¼ teaspoon Worcestershire sauce
¼ teaspoon tabasco sauce

Remove flesh from Balmain bugs, cut each piece in half lengthways. Place lettuce, onion, cucumber, apple and flesh in 4 serving dishes, sprinkle with juice and top with sauce just before serving.

Cocktail Sauce: Combine mayonnaise, cream and sauces in small bowl.
Serves 4.

SEAFOOD SPINACH TERRINE

We used redfish fillets in this recipe. You will need 1 bunch of English spinach (40 leaves) or about 6 large silverbeet leaves. With stems removed, cut green parts into 5cm pieces for terrine and sauce. Terrine can be made 2 days ahead; keep, covered, in refrigerator. This recipe is not suitable to freeze or microwave.

- 20 English spinach leaves
- ¼ cup water
- ¼ cup dry white wine
- 400g white fish fillets
- 1 tablespoon gelatine
- ¼ cup water, extra
- 2 tablespoons chopped fresh chives
- ¼ cup cream
- ¼ cup lemon juice
- 400g smoked trout
- 200g butter
- 2 tablespoons cream, extra
- 1 tablespoon lemon juice, extra

SPINACH HERB DRESSING
- 20 English spinach leaves
- ¼ cup chopped fresh parsley
- ¼ cup chopped fresh chives
- ½ cup water
- 2 egg yolks
- 1 teaspoon French mustard
- 1½ tablespoons lemon juice
- 1 cup oil
- 1 tablespoon hot water

Lightly oil 8cm x 26cm loaf pan, line with plastic wrap. Boil, steam or microwave spinach until wilted, rinse under cold water, pat dry with absorbent paper.

Add water and wine to small frying pan, bring to boil, reduce heat, add white fish fillets, simmer, uncovered, for about 2 minutes or until cooked; drain and cool.

Sprinkle gelatine over extra water in small bowl, stand in small pan of simmering water, stir constantly until gelatine is dissolved.

Blend or process white fish fillets until smooth, transfer to medium bowl, stir in chives, cream, juice and gelatine.

Remove flesh from smoked trout, discard any bones and skin. Blend or process with butter, extra cream and extra juice until smooth.

Spread half the smoked trout filling into dish, top with spinach leaves, then spread with white fish filling. Top with spinach leaves then remaining smoked trout filling. Cover, refrigerate overnight. Serve with dressing.

Spinach Herb Dressing: Place spinach, parsley, chives and water in medium saucepan. Bring to boil, reduce heat, simmer, covered, for 10 minutes. Drain spinach mixture; cool. Blend or process egg yolks, mustard and juice until smooth. Add oil gradually in thin stream while motor is operating, add water and spinach mixture; blend until combined.

LEFT: Seafood Spinach Terrine.
ABOVE: Balmain Bug Cocktails.

CUTTLEFISH WITH TAMARIND LEMON GRASS SAUCE

Sauce can be prepared several hours ahead of serving; cuttlefish must be prepared just before serving. Recipe unsuitable to freeze or microwave.

750g cuttlefish
⅓ cup plain flour
1 teaspoon paprika
2 tablespoons oil
TAMARIND LEMON GRASS SAUCE
1 lemon grass stem
2 cloves garlic, finely chopped
1 tablespoon lime juice
1½ tablespoons hoisin sauce
1 teaspoon anchovy sauce
1½ tablespoons tamarind sauce

Cut inside of cuttlefish in diamond pattern; do not cut right through. Then cut into 1cm strips. Toss cuttlefish in combined flour and paprika, shake away excess flour.

Heat half the oil in large frying pan until very hot. Add half the cuttlefish, stir-fry over high heat for about 30 seconds or until lightly browned and tender, drain on absorbent paper. Repeat with remaining oil and cuttlefish. Serve with sauce.

Tamarind Lemon Grass Sauce: Remove tough outer leaves from lemon grass, chop in half, discard woody centre. Coarsely chop tender white part of lemon grass. Blend or process lemon grass, garlic, juice and sauces until finely chopped.

Serves 4.

SQUID IN MUSTARD CREAM

Squid must be cooked just before serving. This recipe is not suitable to freeze or microwave.

500g squid hoods, sliced
¼ cup lemon juice
30g butter
1 tablespoon plain flour
1 small chicken stock cube, crumbled
¼ cup water
½ cup milk
¾ cup thickened cream
1 teaspoon French mustard
2 teaspoons seeded mustard
1 tablespoon chopped fresh dill

Combine squid and lemon juice in medium bowl, cover, refrigerate for 1 hour. Melt butter in large saucepan, add flour, stir constantly over medium heat for 1 minute. Remove from heat, gradually stir in combined stock cube, water, milk and cream; stir constantly over high heat until mixture boils and thickens. Stir in mustards, then squid and lemon mixture, cook for about 2 minutes or until squid is tender, then stir in dill.

Serves 6.

SQUID WITH NUTTY CHICKEN PATE

Squid can be filled up to a day ahead; keep, covered, in refrigerator. This recipe is not suitable to freeze.

375g chicken breast fillets, chopped
2 tablespoons chopped fresh chives
2 tablespoons chopped fresh parsley
1 tablespoon seeded mustard
130g can creamed corn
1 cup stale breadcrumbs
2 tablespoons chopped fresh basil
¼ cup roasted unsalted cashew nuts, chopped
4 squid hoods (300g)
CREAMED CORN SAUCE
300ml carton cream
130g can creamed corn
1 teaspoon paprika

Blend or process chicken until smooth; combine with chives, parsley, mustard, corn, breadcrumbs, basil and nuts in large bowl. Spoon mixture into squid hoods, secure with toothpicks.

Bring large saucepan of water to boil, add squid, cover, return to boil. Reduce heat, simmer for about 25 minutes (or microwave on MEDIUM for about 12 minutes) or until squid is tender. Stand for 5 minutes, remove toothpicks, cut squid into slices, serve with sauce.

Creamed Corn Sauce: Combine cream, corn and paprika in small saucepan. Bring to boil, reduce heat, simmer, uncovered, for about 10 minutes (or microwave on HIGH for about 5 minutes) or until mixture reduces and thickens slightly. Strain sauce before serving.

Serves 4.

SMOKED EEL PATE

Pâté can be prepared up to 3 days ahead; keep, covered, in refrigerator. This recipe is not suitable to freeze.

250g smoked eel
60g butter, melted
2 tablespoons chopped fresh chives
2 tablespoons chopped fresh oregano
¼ cup cream

Remove skin and bones from eel. Blend or process eel with butter, herbs and cream until smooth. Divide mixture into 4 dishes (⅓ cup capacity), cover, refrigerate pâté for several hours before serving.

Serves 4.

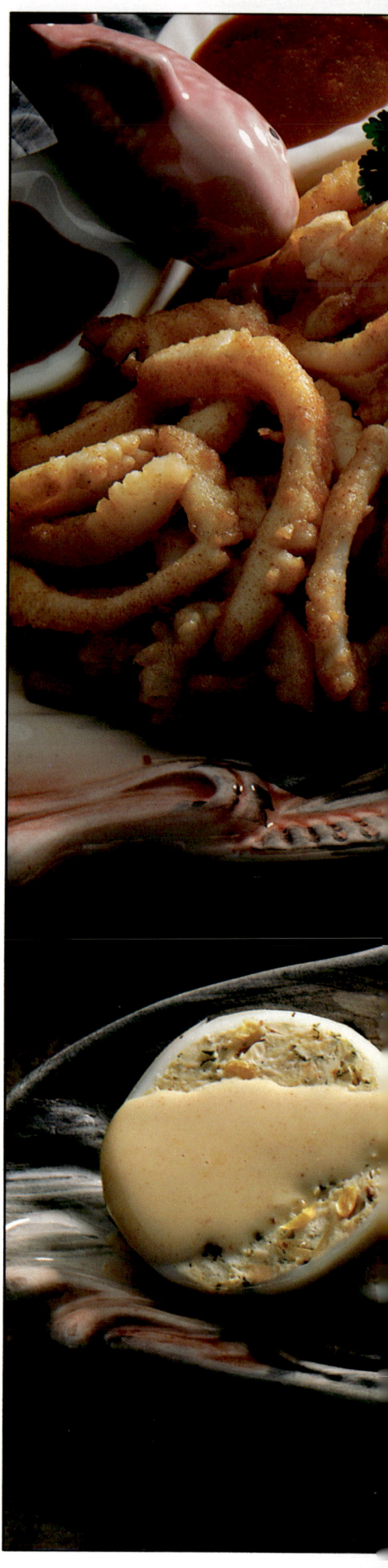

Clockwise from top: Cuttlefish with Tamarind Lemon Grass Sauce; Squid in Mustard Cream; Squid with Nutty Chicken Pâté.

Plates: Villa Italiana

COCKLE AND BROCCOLI SALAD

Cockles can be cooked a day before required; keep, covered, in refrigerator. Prepare the salad just before serving. This recipe is not suitable to freeze.

**1kg cockles
500g broccoli, chopped
2 tablespoons lime juice
1 small onion, finely chopped
1 medium red pepper, sliced
½ teaspoon sugar
150g can coconut cream
1 small fresh red chilli, finely chopped**

Add enough cold water to large saucepan to cover base by 1cm, add cockles, cover, bring to boil, reduce heat, simmer, uncovered, for about 1 minute (or microwave on HIGH for about 1 minute) or until shells are just opened.

Remove flesh from shells, remove and discard beards, cut cockles in half. Boil, steam or microwave broccoli until just tender, drain, cool. Combine cockles, broccoli, juice, onion, pepper, sugar, cream and chilli in serving bowl, refrigerate before serving.

Serves 4.

SEAFOOD SALAD WITH AVOCADO DRESSING

Salad is best prepared just before serving. We used ling fish. This recipe is not suitable to freeze.

**500g cooked king prawns
1½ tablespoons lime juice
½ cup dry white wine
2 tablespoons chopped fresh dill
125g white fish fillets, sliced
125g scallops
125 mussel meat
½ x 250 punnet cherry tomatoes
1 small lettuce**
AVOCADO DRESSING
**1 medium avocado
1 small onion, chopped
1½ tablespoons lime juice
2 teaspoons olive oil**

Shell and devein prawns, leaving tails intact. Combine juice, wine and dill in small frying pan, bring to boil, reduce heat, add fish, scallops and mussels. Simmer for about 2 minutes or until seafood is just cooked. Drain (discard liquid), cool seafood, then refrigerate, covered, before completing salad. Combine seafood, tomatoes and lettuce in bowl, toss lightly, top with dressing just before serving.

Avocado Dressing: Blend or process in ingredients until smooth.

Serves 4.

HOT ANCHOVY DIP

Dip can be made up to a day ahead; keep, covered, in refrigerator. Reheat just before serving. This recipe is not suitable to freeze.

**15g butter
1 clove garlic, crushed
45g can anchovy fillets
300ml carton cream
3 teaspoons cornflour
¼ cup water**

Melt butter in small saucepan, add garlic, cook for 1 minute; do not brown (or microwave on HIGH for about 1 minute). Add undrained anchovies and cream, bring to boil, reduce heat, simmer, uncovered, for 5 minutes (or microwave on HIGH for about 10 minutes).

Blend cornflour with water, stir into anchovy mixture, stir constantly over high heat (or microwave on HIGH for about 1 minute) or until mixture boils and thickens. Serve hot with vegetables of your choice.

Serves 4.

RIGHT: Top: Seafood Salad with Avocado Dressing; below: Cockle and Broccoli Salad. ABOVE: Top: Smoked Eel Pâté; below: Hot Anchovy Dip.

PICKLED OCTOPUS WITH CUCUMBER VINAIGRETTE

Recipe is best prepared a day ahead; keep, covered, in refrigerator. This recipe is not suitable to freeze or microwave.

**12 baby octopus
2 long thin green cucumbers, sliced
½ cup dry white wine
¼ cup lime juice
2 tablespoons lemon juice
1 cup white vinegar
2 tablespoons sugar
1 teaspoon sambal oelek
½ teaspoon yellow mustard seeds
½ teaspoon dill seeds
1 teaspoon cracked black pepper
2 tablespoons olive oil
1 tablespoon chopped fresh dill
2 tablespoons chopped fresh coriander**

Remove heads and beaks from octopus. Combine octopus, cucumbers, wine, juices, vinegar, sugar, sambal oelek, seeds and pepper in large bowl; mix well, cover, refrigerate overnight.

Strain octopus and cucumber from marinade, place marinade in large saucepan, bring to boil. Add octopus and cucumber, remove pan from heat, cool to room temperature. Drain octopus and cucumber, reserve 1 cup liquid. Place octopus, cucumber and reserved liquid in medium bowl, add oil, dill and coriander; cover, refrigerate several hours before serving.

Serves 4.

SQUID AND TOMATO SALAD

This recipe is not suitable to freeze or microwave.

**500g small squid hoods, sliced
1 teaspoon oil
1 medium onion, chopped
1 clove garlic, crushed
2 small fresh red chillies, chopped
410g can tomatoes
1 small chicken stock cube, crumbled
¼ cup water
2 teaspoons castor sugar
24 black olives, pitted
1 small lettuce
1 small cucumber, sliced
1 tablespoon chopped fresh basil**

Drop squid into saucepan of boiling water, boil for about 30 seconds (or microwave on HIGH for about 15 seconds) or until squid are opaque. Drain, rinse under cold water.

Heat oil in frying pan, add onion, garlic and chillies, stir constantly over medium heat until onion is soft. Stir in undrained crushed tomatoes, stock cube, water and sugar. Bring to boil, reduce heat, simmer, uncovered, for about 8 minutes, or until mixture thickens slightly. Add olives, cool to room temperature. Stir in squid, serve with lettuce and cucumber, sprinkle with basil.

Serves 4.

BELOW: Left: Squid and Tomato Salad; right: Pickled Octopus with Cucumber Vinaigrette. RIGHT: Fish Paupiettes with Lemon Pepper Sauce.

FISH PAUPIETTES WITH LEMON PEPPER SAUCE

We used sole fillets in this recipe. Prepare the dish as close to serving time as possible. Completed recipe is not suitable to freeze or microwave.

20 English spinach leaves
12 small white fish fillets
½ cup dry white wine
½ cup water
paprika
LEMON PEPPER SAUCE
15g butter
1 small onion, chopped
1 clove garlic, crushed
2 medium red peppers, chopped
2 teaspoons chopped fresh thyme
1¼ cups water
1 small chicken stock cube, crumbled
1 teaspoon castor sugar
2 tablespoons lemon juice

Boil, steam or microwave spinach until tender, drain; cool. Squeeze excess moisture from spinach. Place fish on flat surface, divide and spread spinach evenly over fish. Roll up fish, secure with toothpicks.

Combine wine and water in large frying pan, bring to boil, reduce heat, add fish, simmer, uncovered, for about 10 minutes (or microwave on HIGH for about 6 minutes). Serve with sauce, sprinkle with paprika.

Lemon Pepper Sauce: Melt butter in saucepan, add onion, garlic and peppers, stir constantly over heat until onion is soft. Add thyme, water, stock cube, sugar and juice; bring to boil, reduce heat, simmer, uncovered, for about 15 minutes or until peppers are soft. Blend or process until smooth; strain. Reheat before serving.

Serves 6.

SMOKED TROUT TIMBALES WITH RED PEPPER SAUCE

Timbales are best prepared just before serving. Sauce can be prepared up to a day ahead; keep, covered, in refrigerator. This recipe is unsuitable to freeze or microwave.

1 smoked trout (250g)
125g packet cream cheese
1 egg
1 egg yolk
1 tablespoon lemon juice
50g smoked salmon, chopped
⅓ cup cream
RED PEPPER SAUCE
30g butter
1 medium onion, chopped
2 medium red peppers, chopped
1 tablespoon plain flour
1½ cups water
½ large vegetable stock cube, crumbled

Remove skin and bones from trout; flake flesh. Blend or process cheese, egg, egg yolk, juice, trout and salmon until just combined; fold in cream. Divide into 4 greased dishes (½ cup capacity), cover with greased foil.

Place dishes in shallow baking dish, pour enough boiling water into baking dish to come halfway up sides of dishes. Bake in moderate oven for about 40 minutes or until firm. Turn timbales onto serving dishes, serve with sauce.

Red Pepper Sauce: Melt butter in medium saucepan, add onion and peppers, cook over low heat for about 10 minutes, stirring occasionally, until peppers are soft. Add flour, stir constantly over heat for 1 minute. Remove from heat, gradually stir in water and stock cube, stir constantly over high heat until mixture boils and thickens. Blend or process until smooth, strain. Reheat without boiling.

Serves 4.

OYSTER FRITTERS WITH LEMON MUSTARD MAYONNAISE

Serve fritters as soon as they are cooked. Mayonnaise can be made up to 2 days ahead; keep, covered, in refrigerator. This recipe is not suitable to freeze or microwave.

24 oysters
2 tablespoons lemon juice
2 tablespoons plain flour
2 tablespoons self-raising flour
¼ teaspoon bicarbonate of soda
½ cup water
1 egg white
oil for deep-frying
LEMON MUSTARD MAYONNAISE
¾ cup mayonnaise
2 green shallots, chopped
2 tablespoons chopped fresh parsley
½ teaspoon grated lemon rind
1 tablespoon lemon juice
1 teaspoon seeded mustard

Combine oysters and lemon juice in bowl, stand for 15 minutes; drain well.

Sift flours and soda into medium bowl, gradually stir in water, mix to a smooth batter (up to this stage can be done in a blender or processor). Beat egg white in small bowl until soft peaks form, gently fold into batter. Dip oysters into batter, deep-fry a few at a time in hot oil until golden brown. Drain on absorbent paper. Keep cooked oysters warm while frying remaining oysters. Serve with mayonnaise.

Lemon Mustard Mayonnaise: Combine all ingredients in small bowl.

Serves 4.

ABOVE: Oyster Fritters with Lemon Mustard Mayonnaise. BELOW: Smoked Trout Timbales with Red Pepper Sauce. RIGHT: Sashimi with Orange Ginger Dressing.

SASHIMI WITH ORANGE GINGER DRESSING

Tuna should be purchased fresh and served as soon as possible. Dressing can be made up to 2 days ahead; keep, covered, in refrigerator. This recipe is not suitable to freeze.

250g piece tuna fillet
1 bunch chives
1 small daikon, sliced
preserved or pickled ginger
ORANGE GINGER DRESSING
⅓ cup orange juice
½ teaspoon sugar
¼ teaspoon English mustard
½ teaspoon grated orange rind
1 teaspoon grated fresh ginger
2 teaspoons Japanese soy sauce

Remove and discard skin and any dark parts from tuna. Slice tuna as thinly as possible. Pour boiling water over about 16 chives, soak for about 1 minute to soften; drain. Roll tuna up, tie with a chive. Place tuna rolls on serving plates, top with dressing, decorate with chives, daikon and ginger.

Orange Ginger Dressing: Combine juice and sugar in small saucepan, bring to boil, reduce heat, simmer, uncovered, for 5 minutes or until reduced to about half. Stir in mustard, rind, ginger and sauce, cool; strain before using.

Serves 4.

SEAFOOD RAVIOLI WITH VERMOUTH

Filling can be made a day ahead; keep, covered, in refrigerator. Ravioli can be made up to 2 days ahead; keep, covered, in refrigerator or freeze for up to 2 months. Sauce is best made just before serving. This recipe is not suitable to microwave.

RAVIOLI DOUGH
2 cups plain flour
1 egg, lightly beaten
2 teaspoons oil
⅓ cup water, approximately
PRAWN FILLING
400g cooked shelled prawns
1 tablespoon chopped fresh dill
2 teaspoons dry vermouth
¼ cup cream
SALMON AND DILL SAUCE
2 x 300ml cartons cream
½ large vegetable stock cube, crumbled
1½ tablespoons dry vermouth
1 teaspoon cornflour
1 teaspoon water
90g smoked salmon, sliced
3 teaspoons chopped fresh dill

Roll ravioli dough out, half at a time, to a thickness of 2mm, cut into 8cm strips (or roll out with a pasta machine). Cover strips with a tea-towel to prevent drying out.

Place heaped teaspoons of prawn filling at 4cm intervals along 1 side of strips of dough. Brush edges with a little water, fold dough over filling; press firmly around filling. Cut between mounds of filling using knife or fluted pastry cutter.

Add ravioli gradually to large saucepan of boiling water, boil, uncovered, for about 8 minutes or until ravioli are cooked; drain. Mix ravioli gently through sauce, serve with grated parmesan cheese, if desired.

Ravioli Dough: Sift flour into large bowl, make well in centre, gradually stir in combined egg, oil and enough water, to make dough firm and pliable. Turn onto lightly floured surface, knead for 5 minutes. Place in lightly oiled bowl, cover, stand for 30 minutes before rolling.

Prawn Filling: Mince, process or blend prawns with dill and vermouth until smooth. Transfer to large bowl, stir in cream gently, cover, refrigerate.

Salmon and Dill Sauce: Combine cream and stock cube in medium saucepan, bring to boil, reduce heat, simmer for about 5 minutes or until mixture is reduced by half. Add vermouth and cornflour blended with water, stir constantly over high heat until mixture boils and thickens, stir in salmon and dill.

Serves 6.

Plate: Villa Italiana

SALMON PITHIVIERS WITH PEPPER BEARNAISE

Ocean trout can be substituted for the salmon in this recipe, if preferred. Pithiviers can be assembled ready for cooking up to 2 hours beforehand; keep, covered, in refrigerator. Recipe unsuitable to freeze or microwave.

200g fresh salmon
200g uncooked prawns, shelled
2 egg whites
¾ cup cream
2 teaspoons chopped fresh dill
2 teaspoons canned drained green peppercorns
3 sheets ready-rolled puff pastry
1 egg yolk
1 tablespoon milk
PEPPER BEARNAISE
2 egg yolks
2 teaspoons tarragon vinegar
200g butter, melted
1 teaspoon canned drained green peppercorns, crushed
3 teaspoons water, approximately

Mince, process or blend salmon and prawns until smooth, add 1 of the egg whites, process until combined. Place in medium bowl, stir in cream, dill and peppercorns. Beat remaining egg white in small bowl until firm peaks form, gently fold into salmon mixture.

Using 9cm and 10cm cutters, cut 6 rounds of each size from pastry sheets. Divide salmon mixture between the 9cm rounds, brush edges lightly with combined egg yolk and milk, top with 10cm rounds, press edges together gently. Using sharp knife, mark tops of pastry rounds as pictured; do not cut all the way through the pastry.

Place pithiviers on lightly greased oven tray, brush lightly with egg mixture, bake in hot oven for 10 minutes. Reduce heat to moderate, bake further 10 minutes or until golden brown. Serve with bearnaise.

Pepper Bearnaise: Combine egg yolks and vinegar in medium bowl or in top half of double saucepan, place over saucepan of simmering water. Whisk constantly over simmering water until thick; remove from heat. Gradually whisk in hot bubbly butter in a thin steady stream. Whisk in peppercorns and enough water to make a pourable consistency.

Makes 6.

RIGHT: Salmon Pithiviers with Pepper Bearnaise. ABOVE RIGHT: Fish and Pepper Satays. ABOVE: Seafood Ravioli with Vermouth.

FISH AND PEPPER SATAYS

We used gemfish in this recipe. Fish can be marinated in satay sauce for up to a day. This recipe is not suitable to freeze or microwave.

**500g white fish fillets, chopped
1 medium red pepper, chopped**
SATAY SAUCE
**¼ cup roasted salted peanuts
1 medium onion, chopped
¼ cup smooth peanut butter
1 clove garlic, crushed
2 tablespoons fruit chutney
2 tablespoons oil
2 teaspoons light soy sauce
¼ cup water
2 tablespoons lemon juice
1 small fresh red chilli, finely chopped**

Thread fish and pepper onto about 8 skewers, place skewers in single layer in dish, top with satay sauce. Cover, refrigerate for several hours or overnight; turn occasionally.

Remove satays from sauce, reserve sauce. Grill or barbecue satays until fish is tender. While fish is cooking, heat reserved sauce ready for serving.
Satay Sauce: Blend or process peanuts and onion until finely chopped. Add remaining ingredients, process until smooth.

Serves 4.

BALMAIN BUGS IN PUFF PASTRY CASES

Pastry cases can be made up to 3 days ahead; keep in an airtight container. Warm cases in oven just before serving. This recipe is not suitable to freeze or microwave.

1 sheet ready-rolled puff pastry
1 egg yolk
1 tablespoon milk
8 cooked Balmain bugs
WATERCRESS SAUCE
2 teaspoons butter
2 teaspoons plain flour
1½ tablespoons dry white wine
¼ cup chopped fresh watercress
½ small onion, chopped
1 cup cream
¼ large vegetable stock cube, crumbled
1 tablespoon chopped fresh watercress, extra

Cut pastry sheet into quarters. On each quarter, cut 1½cm border around 2 opposite corners, leaving about 1cm uncut at each remaining corner.

Lift and fold the 2 cut-out corners to opposite corners (as shown above right). Repeat with remaining pastry.

Place on lightly greased oven tray, brush lightly with combined egg yolk and milk, bake in hot oven for about 10 minutes or until golden brown. Remove flesh from Balmain bugs, cut flesh in half lengthways. Combine flesh and sauce, then spoon into warmed pastry cases. Serve with warm sauce.

Watercress Sauce: Blend soft butter with flour in small bowl until smooth. Combine wine, watercress and onion in small saucepan, cook over low heat for 2 minutes or until onion is soft, add cream, bring to boil. Stir butter mixture into cream mixture with stock cube, stir constantly over high heat until mixture boils and thickens. Add extra watercress, blend or process until smooth.

Serves 4.

SEAFOOD IN CRISP PASTRY PARCELS

Marinara mix consists of different types of seafood, usually squid, fish, prawns, mussels and octopus, etc. Filling for parcels can be prepared up to a day ahead; keep, covered, in refrigerator. This recipe is not suitable to freeze.

60g butter
2 green shallots, chopped
1 clove garlic, crushed
2 teaspoons chopped fresh basil
250g marinara mix
2 tablespoons plain flour
1 cup cream
2 tablespoons dry sherry
8 sheets fillo pastry
60g butter, melted, extra

Melt butter in large saucepan, add shallots, garlic and basil, stir constantly over heat for about 2 minutes (or microwave on HIGH for 1 minute). Stir marinara mix into pan, stir for 3 minutes (or microwave on MEDIUM HIGH for 2 minutes). Add flour to pan, stir constantly over heat until combined (or microwave on MEDIUM HIGH for about 1 minute).

PIPIS WITH ORANGE HERB BUTTER

Pipis must be served immediately they are cooked. This recipe is not suitable to freeze.

¼ cup water
1kg pipis
ORANGE HERB BUTTER
⅔ cup orange juice
185g butter, chopped
2 tablespoons chopped fresh parsley
2 teaspoons chopped fresh oregano
2 teaspoons chopped fresh dill

Heat water in large saucepan, add washed and drained pipis. Cover, cook over high heat (or microwave on MEDIUM for about 6 minutes) or until pipis open; stir occasionally. Lift pipis from water, place on serving plates, top with hot orange herb butter.

Orange Herb Butter: Place orange juice in medium saucepan, bring to boil, add butter, stir until melted (or microwave on HIGH for 1 minute). Stir in herbs.

Serves 4.

BELOW: Pipis with Orange Herb Butter.
LEFT: Seafood in Crisp Pastry Parcels.
FAR LEFT: Balmain Bugs in Puff Pastry Cases.

Gradually stir in cream and sherry, stir constantly over high heat (or microwave on MEDIUM HIGH for about 3 minutes) or until mixture boils and thickens. Cover surface of mixture with plastic to prevent skin forming, cool to room temperature.

Layer 4 sheets of pastry together, brushing each with melted extra butter, then placing the next sheet on top. Repeat with remaining pastry. Cut the 2 pieces of layered pastry in half.

Place a quarter of cooled mixture in centre of each piece of layered pastry. Draw each corner of pastry up and twist each to form a rope. Wrap ropes around top of parcels. Place parcels onto oven trays, brush all over with butter. Bake in moderately hot oven for about 15 minutes or until browned.

Makes 4.

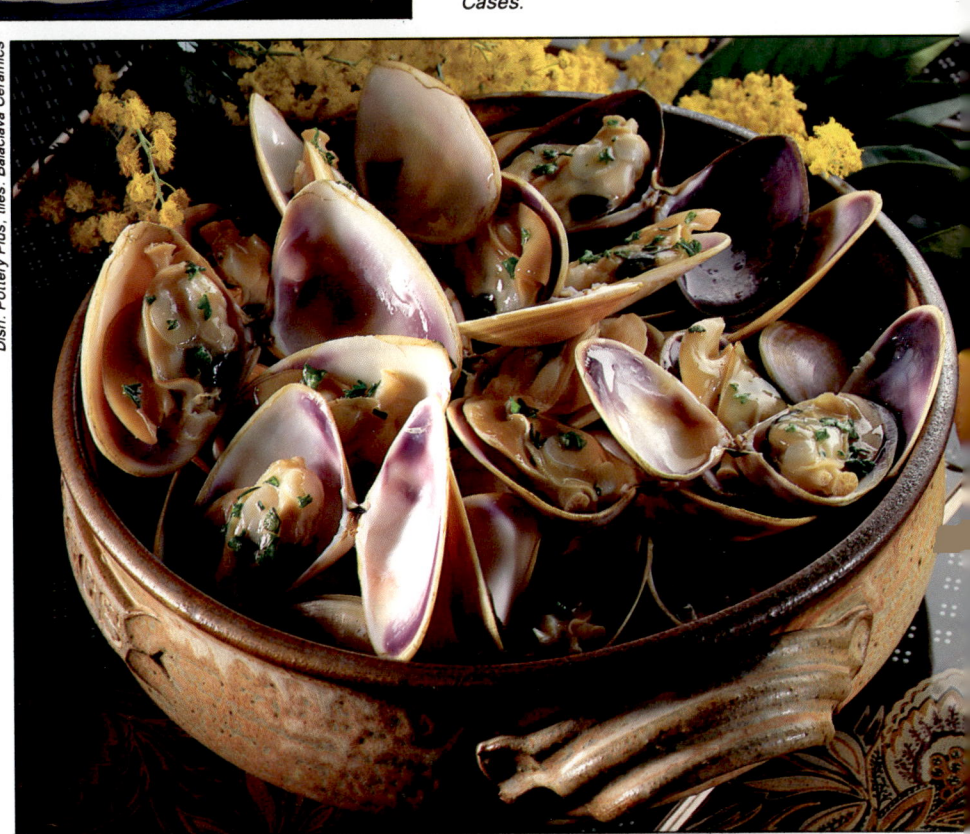

Dish: Pottery Plus; tiles: Balaclava Ceramics

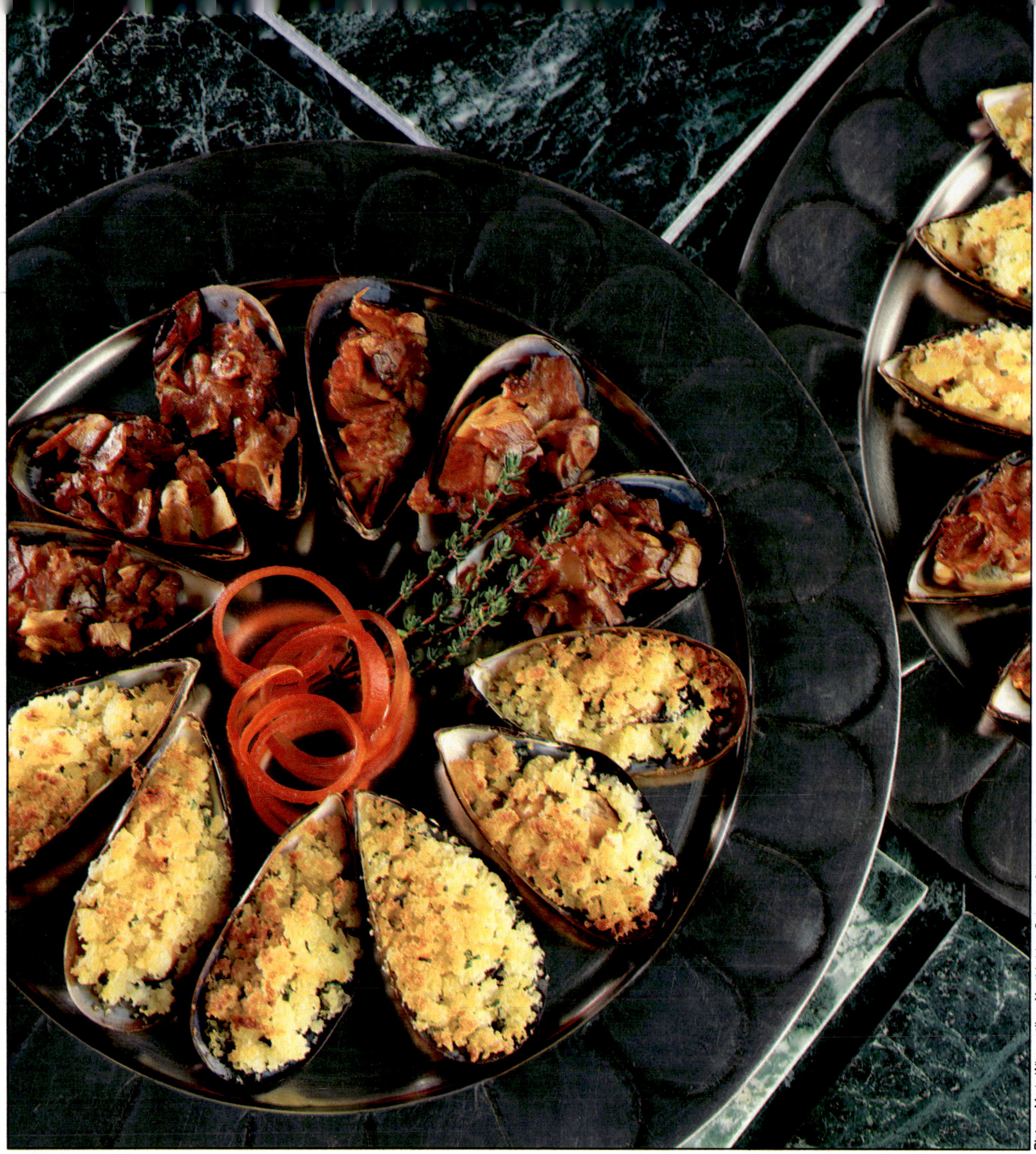

Plates: Made Where; tiles: Northbridge Ceramic & Marble Centre

MUSSELS WITH TWO TOPPINGS

Serve mussels immediately after grilling. This recipe is not suitable to freeze or microwave.

24 mussels
½ cup water
BACON TOPPING
4 bacon rashers, chopped
⅓ cup Japanese soy sauce
GARLIC TOPPING
1½ cups stale breadcrumbs
2 cloves garlic, crushed
2 tablespoons chopped fresh chives
60g butter, melted

Scrub mussels and remove beards. Combine mussels and water in large saucepan, bring to boil, add mussels, cook for about 1½ minutes. Remove mussels from pan as soon as shells open: discard any unopened shells. Loosen mussel meat in shells. Top half the mussels with bacon mixture and the other half with garlic mixture. Grill for about 5 minutes or until toppings are lightly browned.

Bacon Topping: Combine bacon and sauce in small bowl, cover, refrigerate for 2 hours or overnight.

Garlic Topping: Combine breadcrumbs, garlic, chives and butter in small bowl.

Serves 4.

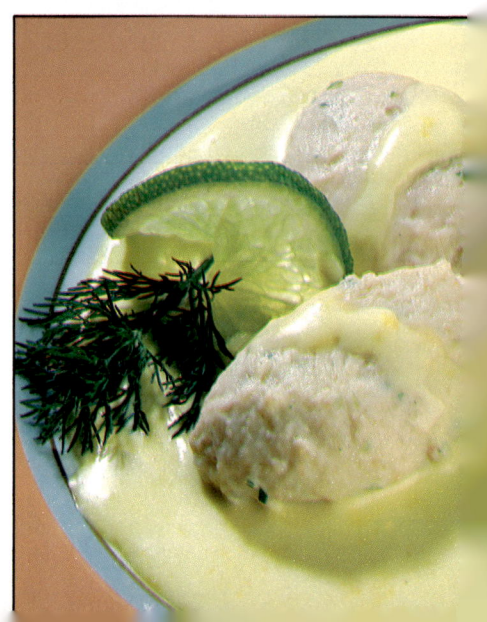

SCALLOP AND PRAWN QUENELLES

Quenelle mixture and sauce can be prepared up to a day ahead; keep, covered, in refrigerator. This recipe is not suitable to freeze or microwave.

250g uncooked prawns, shelled
250g scallops
¼ cup cream
¼ cup sour cream
2 green shallots, coarsely chopped
1 teaspoon grated lemon rind
CREAM SAUCE
60g butter
1 small onion, chopped
¼ cup chopped fresh parsley
1 bay leaf
1 teaspoon chopped fresh rosemary
1 stick celery, chopped
¾ cup water
300ml carton cream
tiny pinch ground saffron

Process all ingredients until smooth. Spread evenly onto flat plate, cover, refrigerate for about 2 hours (or overnight) or until mixture is firm. Mould mixture into oval shapes by using 2 wet dessertspoons.

Drop quenelles into large frying pan with 3cm of simmering water. Simmer for 3 minutes on each side; turn carefully. Do not boil water or quenelles will fall apart. Remove quenelles with slotted spoon to absorbent paper Serve with sauce.

Cream Sauce: Heat butter in medium saucepan, add onion, parsley, bay leaf, rosemary and celery, stir over medium heat for about 3 minutes or until onion is soft. Add water, bring to boil, reduce heat, simmer, uncovered, for about 10 minutes or until reduced by half; strain, return to pan, add cream and saffron. Bring to boil, reduce heat, simmer about 10 minutes or until mixture thickens slightly.

Serves 6.

LOBSTER MEDALLIONS WITH CREAMY PEPPERCORN SAUCE

We used tomato-flavoured fettucine in this recipe. Prepare lobster and sauce just before serving. This recipe is not suitable to freeze or microwave.

1 cup dry white wine
1 cup water
2 tablespoons port
1 tablespoon canned drained green peppercorns
½ cup cream
½ teaspoon French mustard
½ large vegetable stock cube, crumbled
1 tablespoon cornflour
2 tablespoons water, extra
2 small cooked lobsters
375g pasta

Combine wine, water, port and peppercorns in small saucepan, bring to boil, reduce heat, simmer, uncovered, for about 15 minutes or until mixture is reduced by about half. Stir in cream, mustard and stock cube, simmer for 5 minutes.

Blend cornflour with extra water in small bowl, add to mixture, stir constantly over high heat until the sauce boils and thickens.

Remove lobster flesh from shells in 1 piece; slice lobster crossways. Add lobster to sauce, reheat gently without boiling the mixture.

Add pasta to large saucepan of boiling water, boil rapidly, uncovered, until pasta is just tender; drain. Add hot sauce to hot pasta.

Serves 4.

LOBSTER MEDALLIONS WITH MACADAMIA BASIL SAUCE

Prepare lobster and sauce just before serving. This recipe is not suitable to freeze or microwave.

2 small uncooked lobsters
90g butter
1 clove garlic, finely chopped
1 tablespoon chopped macadamia nuts
2 tablespoons tomato paste
3 teaspoons lemon juice
¾ cup dry white wine
2 teaspoons honey
1 tablespoon chopped fresh basil

Remove lobster flesh from shells in 1 piece; slice lobster crossways.

Heat butter in large frying pan, add garlic and nuts, stir constantly over medium heat for about 1 minute or until nuts are lightly browned. Stir in paste, juice, wine and honey. Bring wine mixture to boil. Add lobster in single layer, reduce heat, simmer for about 1 minute on each side or until lobster is tender. Place lobster onto plates, add basil to sauce, pour sauce over lobster.

Serves 4.

ABOVE: From top: Lobster Medallions with Creamy Peppercorn Sauce; Lobster Medallions with Macadamia Basil Sauce. LEFT: Scallop and Prawn Quenelles. FAR LEFT: Top: Mussels with Bacon Topping; bottom: Mussels with Garlic Topping.

PRAWN AND MUSHROOM CREPE CORNETS

Crêpes should be served as soon as they are filled. Filling can be prepared a day ahead; keep, covered, in refrigerator. Crêpes can be frozen for 2 months, layered with freezer or plastic wrap. This recipe is not suitable to microwave.

CREPES
¼ cup plain flour
1 egg, lightly beaten
½ teaspoon oil
⅓ cup milk
PRAWN FILLING
30g butter
2 tablespoons plain flour
1½ cups water
1 small chicken stock cube, crumbled
500g cooked prawns, shelled, chopped
125g baby mushrooms, sliced
2 tablespoons dry white wine
¼ cup cream
1 tablespoon chopped fresh dill

Crêpes: Sift flour into bowl, make well in centre. Gradually stir in combined egg, oil and milk, stir until batter is smooth. (Mixture can be made by blending or processing all ingredients until smooth.) Strain batter into jug, stand for 30 minutes.

Heat heavy-based crêpe pan over medium heat, grease with small knob of butter. Pour 2 to 3 tablespoons batter into pan, swirling batter to cover base of pan evenly. When crêpe is lightly browned underneath, carefully turn with spatula or fingers, lightly brown other side. Repeat with remaining batter to make 4 crêpes.

Grease the outside of 4 cream horn tins, wrap crêpes around tins, place onto oven tray. Bake in moderate oven for about 5 minutes or until firm. Remove crêpes from tray, remove tins, fill crêpes with prawn mixture.

Prawn Filling: Melt butter in medium saucepan, add flour, stir constantly over heat for 1 minute. Remove from heat, stir in water and stock cube, stir constantly over high heat until mixture boils and thickens. Add prawns, mushrooms, wine, cream and dill; reheat gently without boiling.

Serves 4.

SALMON CREPE ROLLUPS

Crêpes can be made several hours before required or can be frozen for 2 months, layered with freezer or plastic wrap. Rollups can be prepared several hours before serving. Sauce must be made just before serving. This recipe is not suitable to freeze or microwave.

CREPES
¾ cup plain flour
3 eggs, lightly beaten
1 tablespoon oil
1 cup milk
SALMON FILLING
250g packet cream cheese
¼ cup lemon juice
210g can red salmon, drained
LIME BUTTER SAUCE
3 egg yolks
1 teaspoon grated lime rind
2 tablespoons lime juice
1 tablespoon French dressing
185g butter
1 tablespoon chopped fresh dill

Crêpes: Sift flour into bowl, make well in centre. Gradually stir in combined eggs, oil and milk, stir until batter is smooth. (Mixture can be made by blending or processing all ingredients until smooth.) Strain batter into jug, stand for 30 minutes.

Heat heavy-based crêpe pan over medium heat, grease with small knob of butter. Pour 2 to 3 tablespoons batter into pan, swirling batter to cover base of pan evenly. When crêpe is lightly browned underneath, carefully turn with spatula or fingers, brown other side. Repeat with remaining batter to make about 12 crêpes.

Spread half the crêpes with salmon filling, top with remaining crêpes, roll up carefully, wrap in greaseproof paper or plastic wrap, refrigerate for 1 hour. Remove paper from crêpes, slice, serve with sauce.

Salmon Filling: Blend or process cheese and lemon juice until smooth, add salmon, blend until smooth.

Lime Butter Sauce: Combine egg yolks, rind, juice and dressing in top of double saucepan, stir constantly over simmering water for 1 minute. Gradually whisk in small pieces of softened butter, whisk until sauce thickens. Remove from heat, stir in dill.

Serves 6.

From top: Prawn and Mushroom Crêpe Cornets; Salmon Crêpe Rollups.

SARDINES WITH BASIL AND OLIVE SEASONING

Sardines can be prepared and seasoned a day ahead; keep, covered, in refrigerator. Serve immediately they are cooked. This recipe is not suitable to freeze or microwave.

**12 large sardines
plain flour
2 tablespoons olive oil
90g butter
2 tablespoons chopped fresh basil**
BASIL AND OLIVE SEASONING
**6 pitted black olives, finely chopped
1 clove garlic, crushed
1 tablespoon grated parmesan cheese
2 teaspoons chopped fresh basil
1½ tablespoons chopped canned pimientos**

Remove heads and backbones from sardines. Fill cavity of each sardine with a little of the seasoning. Fold sides together to enclose seasoning. Dust sardines lightly with flour.

Heat oil in large frying pan, add sardines in single layer. Cook over medium heat for about 3 minutes on each side or until sardines are soft to touch; turn once during cooking. Drain on absorbent paper, transfer to hot serving plates.

Heat medium saucepan, add butter, swirl quickly to melt, add basil; spoon immediately over hot sardines.

Basil and Olive Seasoning: Combine olives, garlic, cheese, basil and pimientos in small bowl.

Serves 4 to 6.

SESAME SEED WHITEBAIT

Whitebait are eaten whole; they can be crumbed ready for frying several hours ahead of serving time. Keep, covered, in refrigerator. Serve immediately they are cooked. This recipe is not suitable to freeze or microwave.

**1 cup stale breadcrumbs
½ cup sesame seeds
250g whitebait
plain flour
2 eggs, lightly beaten
oil for deep-frying**

Combine breadcrumbs and sesame seeds in dish. Toss whitebait in flour, shake off excess flour.

Dip whitebait in eggs in dish, toss in breadcrumb mixture. Deep-fry whitebait in hot oil until lightly browned, drain on absorbent paper before serving. Serve with lemon.

Serves 4.

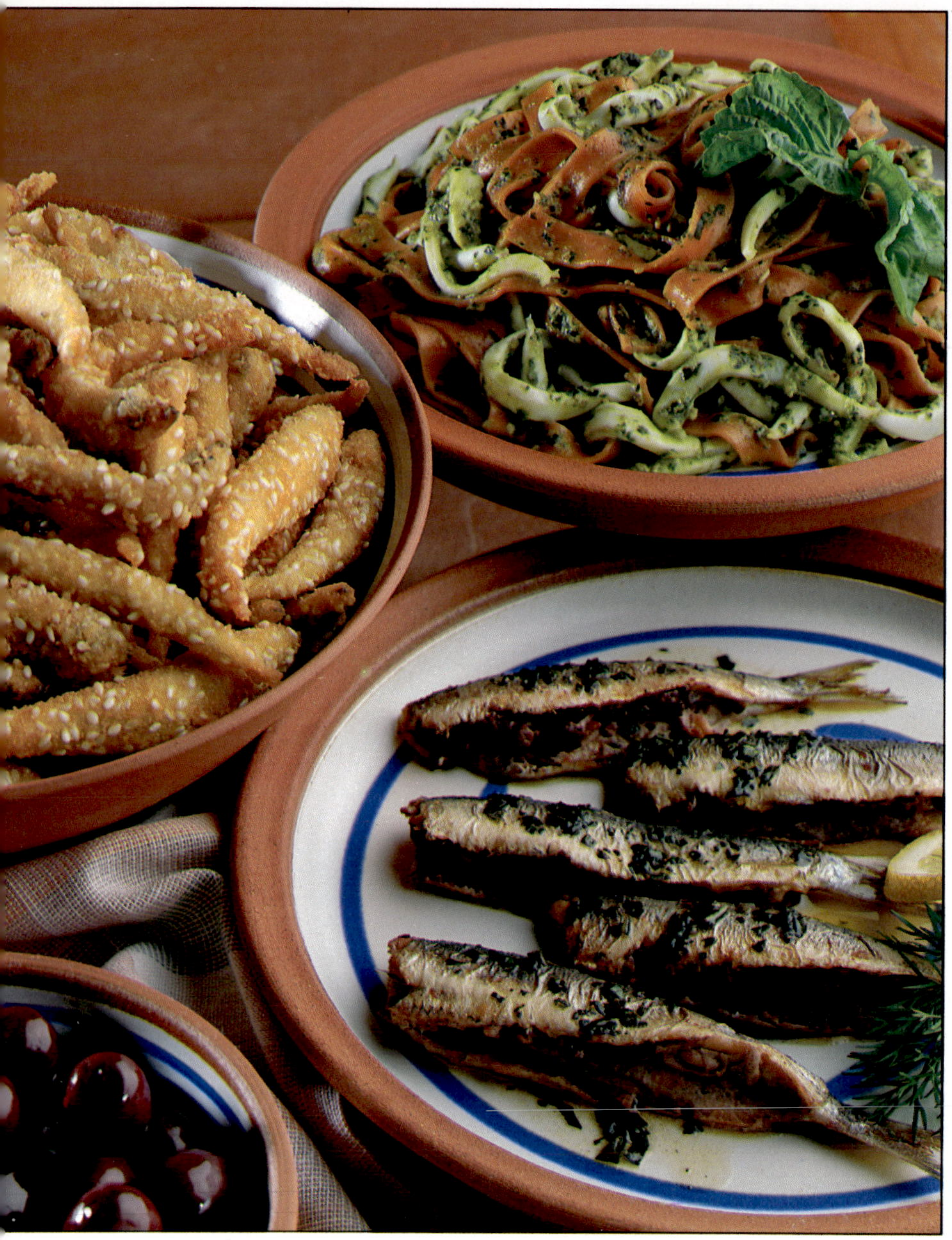

Tiles: Northbridge Ceramic and Marble Centre

PRAWNS IN HERBED TOMATO SAUCE WITH FETA CHEESE

Sauce can be prepared several hours ahead; keep, covered, in refrigerator. Add prawns, herbs and cheese when reheating. This recipe is not suitable to freeze or microwave.

1kg uncooked king prawns
30g butter
1 medium onion, chopped
1 clove garlic, crushed
410g can tomatoes
¼ cup dry white wine
1 tablespoon tomato paste
½ large vegetable stock cube, crumbled
1 teaspoon chopped fresh oregano
125g feta cheese, chopped
2 tablespoons chopped fresh parsley

Shell prawns, leaving tails intact; remove veins. Melt butter in medium frying pan, add onion and garlic, stir constantly over medium heat until onion is soft. Add undrained crushed tomatoes, wine, tomato paste and stock cube; bring to boil, reduce heat, simmer for 10 minutes.

Add prawns, cover, simmer for about 10 minutes or until prawns are cooked. Remove from heat, add oregano and cheese, then half the parsley. Sprinkle with remaining parsley just before serving.

Serves 4.

CUTTLEFISH WITH FETTUCINE AND PESTO

We used fresh tomato-flavoured fettucine in this recipe but any flavour and type of pasta can be used. Pesto can be made up to 2 hours ahead; cover surface with plastic wrap to exclude air. It can also be frozen without cheese for up to 2 months. Add cheese when pesto has thawed, just before using. This recipe is not suitable to microwave.

4 large (500g) cuttlefish
¼ cup lemon juice
250g pasta
PESTO
1 tablespoon olive oil
2 tablespoons pine nuts
2 cups lightly packed fresh basil leaves
2 cloves garlic, chopped
2 tablespoons olive oil, extra
⅓ cup grated fresh parmesan cheese

Cut cuttlefish into thin strips. Combine cuttlefish and lemon juice in bowl, stand for 30 minutes. Cook pasta in large saucepan of boiling water until just tender, drain. Combine pasta, undrained cuttlefish and pesto in large frying pan, stir constantly over medium heat for about 2 minutes or until cuttlefish are tender.

Pesto: Combine oil and pine nuts in small saucepan, stir constantly over medium heat until pine nuts are lightly browned. Blend or process pine nut mixture, basil and garlic until finely chopped. While motor is operating, add extra oil in a thin stream. Transfer mixture to bowl, stir in cheese.

Serves 6.

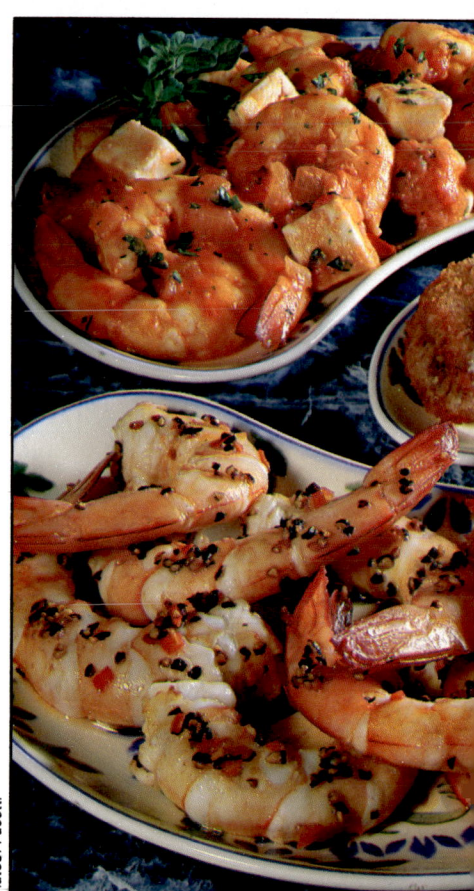

ABOVE: Clockwise from left: Sesame Seed Whitebait; Cuttlefish with Fettucine and Pesto; Sardines with Basil and Olive Seasoning.

Plates: Facetti

PEPPERED GARLIC PRAWNS

Prawns must be cooked just before serving. This recipe is not suitable to freeze or microwave.

**1kg uncooked king prawns
8 cloves garlic, crushed
1 tablespoon cracked black peppercorns
1 small fresh red chilli, finely chopped
2 tablespoons lemon juice
1 cup oil
1 cup olive oil**

Shell prawns, leaving tails intact; remove veins. Combine garlic, peppercorns, chilli, lemon juice and prawns in large bowl, cover, stand for at least 1 hour; refrigerate after 1 hour.

Remove prawns from garlic mixture. Heat both oils in large frying pan, add garlic mixture, cook for 1 minute over high heat. Add prawns; stir gently over high heat until cooked. Remove prawns to serving dishes, top with a little hot oil.

Serves 4.

PRAWNS WITH APRICOT AND PINE NUT SEASONING

Prawns can be seasoned and crumbed up to a day ahead; keep, covered, in refrigerator or freeze for up to a month. This recipe is unsuitable to microwave.

**750g uncooked king prawns
plain flour
1 egg, lightly beaten
⅓ cup milk
2 cups stale breadcrumbs
oil for deep-frying**
APRICOT AND PINE NUT SEASONING
**1 teaspoon oil
2 tablespoons pine nuts
1 tablespoon finely chopped raisins
1 medium glacé apricot, finely chopped
1 teaspoon grated lime rind
2 teaspoons lime juice**
YOGHURT ORANGE MAYONNAISE
**⅓ cup mayonnaise
½ cup plain yoghurt
1 teaspoon grated orange rind
1 tablespoon orange juice**

Peel prawns, leaving tails intact; remove veins. Cover prawns with plastic wrap, placing so back without vein is uppermost. Pound gently with meat mallet until slightly flattened.

Spread each prawn evenly with a heaped teaspoon of seasoning, fold sides over to cover seasoning. Toss in flour; shake away excess flour. Dip in combined egg and milk; toss in breadcrumbs. Deep-fry in hot oil for about 1 minute or until browned; drain on absorbent paper. Serve with yoghurt orange mayonnaise.

Apricot and Pine Nut Seasoning: Heat oil in small frying pan, add nuts, stir constantly over medium heat for about 1 minute or until lightly browned; drain on absorbent paper. Chop nuts finely, combine in small bowl with raisins, apricot, rind and juice.

Yoghurt Orange Mayonnaise: Combine ingredients in medium bowl.

Serves 4.

GRAVLAX

This dish using uncooked fish is traditionally Scandinavian. Use a whole fillet of either Atlantic salmon or ocean trout for this recipe. This recipe is not suitable to freeze.

**375g fish fillet
⅓ cup castor sugar
¼ cup coarse cooking salt
2 tablespoons cracked black peppercorns
⅓ cup chopped fresh dill
⅓ cup chopped fresh chives**
VINAIGRETTE
**¼ cup oil
1 tablespoon white wine vinegar
1 teaspoon lime juice
1 teaspoon cracked black peppercorns
1 tablespoon chopped fresh dill
¼ teaspoon sugar**

Remove skin, bones, fins and any fatty bits from fish.

Combine sugar, salt, peppercorns, dill and chives in small bowl. Sprinkle half the sugar mixture on plastic tray or tray lined with plastic wrap. Place fish on top of sugar mixture and sprinkle remaining sugar mixture over fish. Cover tightly with plastic wrap, refrigerate overnight.

Wash fish quickly and gently under cold water, pat dry with absorbent paper. Slice fish finely. Place fish onto serving plates, top with vinaigrette.

Vinaigrette: Combine oil, vinegar, juice, peppercorns, dill and sugar in jar, shake well.

Serves 4.

ABOVE: Gravlax. LEFT: Clockwise from top: Prawns in Herbed Tomato Sauce with Feta Cheese; Prawns with Apricot and Pine Nut Seasoning; Peppered Garlic Prawns.

SPECIAL OCCASION DISHES

Elegantly presented with fruit, herbs and many unusual flavour combinations, seafood adds style to your smartest dinner party or luncheon. Serve most dishes with seasonal vegetables, salad, rice or pasta.

Plates: Chelsea House Antiques.

PRAWNS WITH GARLIC AND CURRANTS

Prawns are best prepared just before serving This recipe is not suitable to freeze or microwave.

1½kg uncooked king prawns
30g butter
1 clove garlic, chopped
2 tablespoons currants
2 tablespoons Worcestershire sauce
300ml carton thickened cream
½ teaspoon sugar
2 tablespoons chopped fresh parsley

Shell and devein prawns, leaving tails intact. Heat butter in large frying pan until butter begins to brown. Gradually add prawns to pan in single layer, stir constantly over high heat for about 2 minutes or until prawns are just cooked; drain.

Add garlic and currants to remaining butter in pan, stir over medium heat until garlic is lightly browned. Stir in sauce, cream and sugar, bring to boil. Boil for about 3 minutes or until sauce is reduced and thickened slightly. Add parsley and prawns, cook few minutes or until prawns are tender and heated through.

Serves 4.

PAN-FRIED SNAPPER TAILS WITH CREAMED PEPPERS

Cook fish just before serving. Creamed peppers can be prepared up to 2 hours ahead; keep, covered, in refrigerator, reheat without boiling. Recipe unsuitable to freeze or microwave.

4 snapper tails
plain flour
30g butter
2 tablespoons oil
CREAMED PEPPERS
30g butter
2 large red peppers, sliced
½ cup cream

Lightly dust fish with flour, shake off excess flour. Heat butter and oil in large frying pan, add fish in single layer. Cook on each side for about 10 minutes, or until tender; drain on absorbent paper. Serve fish with creamed peppers.

Creamed Peppers: Heat butter in medium saucepan, add peppers, cover, cook over very low heat for about 10 minutes or until peppers are soft, stirring occasionally Stir in cream, simmer for 5 minutes.

Serves 4.

POACHED FISH WITH CITRUS SAUCE

We used John dory in this dish. Recipe is best prepared just before serving. This recipe is unsuitable to freeze or microwave.

4 medium white fish fillets
¼ cup dry white wine
6 black peppercorns
1 bay leaf
1 small onion, sliced
CITRUS SAUCE
1 medium orange
1 tablespoon castor sugar
1 teaspoon cornflour
1 teaspoon water
15g butter

Place fish in single layer in large frying pan with wine, peppercorns, bay leaf and onion, add enough water to just cover fish. Poach over medium heat until fish is tender; remove from pan, drain on absorbent paper. Serve with citrus sauce.

Citrus Sauce: Remove rind from orange using vegetable peeler; cut rind into long thin strips. Squeeze juice from orange; you will need ½ cup juice for this recipe. Place sugar in small saucepan, cook over medium heat, without stirring, until sugar is melted and golden in colour. Add juice, stir until toffee is melted. Blend cornflour and water, stir into sugar mixture, stir over high heat until mixture boils and thickens. Remove from heat, add butter and rind, stir until butter is melted.

Serves 4.

CHUNKY FISH WITH GINGER PEPPERCORN SAUCE

We used ling fillets in this dish. Sauce can be made up to 2 days ahead; keep, covered, in refrigerator. This recipe is not suitable to freeze or microwave.

60g butter
750g white fish fillets
5cm piece fresh ginger, finely sliced
1 teaspoon grated lime rind
2 tablespoons lime juice
½ cup sweet sherry
1 tablespoon brown sugar
2 teaspoons canned drained green peppercorns

Heat butter in large frying pan. Add fish to pan in single layer. Cook for about 3 minutes on each side or until fish is tender. Drain on absorbent paper; keep warm. Reheat remaining butter in pan, add ginger, cook for 1 minute. Stir in rind, juice, sherry, sugar and peppercorns. Bring to boil, reduce heat, simmer, uncovered, for about 15 minutes or until sauce is slightly thickened. Serve with fish.

Serves 4.

ABOVE: From top: Pan-Fried Snapper Tails with Creamed Peppers; Prawns with Garlic and Currants. LEFT: From top: Poached Fish with Citrus Sauce; Chunky Fish with Ginger Peppercorn Sauce.

HONEY LIME LOBSTER WITH AVOCADO CREAM

This recipe is also delicious if uncooked prawns are used instead of lobster; you will need 5 large prawns per person. This recipe is not suitable to freeze or microwave.

4 uncooked lobster tails
30g butter
1 clove garlic, crushed
1 tablespoon lime juice
¼ cup lemon juice
¼ cup dry white wine
1 tablespoon honey
200g vermicelli noodles
2 teaspoons oil
⅓ cup French dressing
2 tablespoons poppy seeds
AVOCADO CREAM
2 egg yolks
1 teaspoon grated lime rind
2 tablespoons lemon juice
125g butter
1 medium avocado
1 tablespoon French dressing
½ cup milk
2 tablespoons sour cream
¼ cup grated fresh parmesan cheese

Remove lobster flesh from shells, cut into 1cm slices. Combine butter, garlic, juices, wine and honey in shallow frying pan. Add lobster, bring to boil, cover, reduce heat, simmer for about 4 minutes or until lobster is tender; drain, discard stock.

Add noodles gradually to large saucepan of boiling water. Add oil, boil rapidly for about 3 minutes or until just tender; drain. Combine dressing and poppy seeds in jug, pour over noodles, mix well. Serve lobster with noodles and avocado cream.

Avocado Cream: Combine egg yolks, rind and lemon juice in top of double saucepan or bowl over simmering water; whisk for 1 minute. Whisk in small pieces of softened butter gradually, whisk over heat until sauce thickens. Blend or process avocado, dressing, milk, sour cream and cheese until smooth. Add hot butter mixture gradually while motor is operating, process until thick.

Serves 4.

PEPPERED FISH WITH LIME BUTTER SAUCE

We used mullet in this recipe. Fish can be marinated up to 2 hours ahead; cook just before serving. This recipe is not suitable to freeze or microwave.

⅓ cup lime juice
¼ cup white wine vinegar
2 green shallots, chopped
1 tablespoon sugar
1 clove garlic, crushed
4 medium oily fish fillets
2 tablespoons cracked black peppercorns
30g butter
½ cup water
100g butter, chopped, extra

Combine lime juice, vinegar, shallots, sugar and garlic in small bowl. Place fish in single layer in shallow dish, pour lime mixture over fish, cover, refrigerate for 2 hours.

Remove fish from marinade, strain, reserve marinade. Pat fish dry with absorbent paper. Sprinkle both sides of fish with peppercorns. Heat butter in large frying pan, add fish in single layer, cook for about 4 minutes on each side or until fish is cooked. Remove fish from pan, keep warm.

Heat marinade in small saucepan, add water, bring to boil, reduce heat, simmer, uncovered, for about 10 minutes or until mixture is reduced by half. Gradually whisk extra butter into sauce over heat. Serve sauce over fish.

Serves 4.

SALMON CUTLETS WITH FRESH HERB SAUCE

Ocean trout can be used instead of salmon in this recipe, if preferred. Cook fish and sauce as close as possible to serving time. This recipe is not suitable to freeze or microwave.

3 cups water
⅓ cup lemon juice
4 medium Atlantic salmon cutlets
FRESH HERB SAUCE
1 cup thickened cream
¼ cup dry vermouth
2 teaspoons lemon juice
3 green shallots, chopped
1 small clove garlic, crushed
1 tablespoon drained capers
1 teaspoon chopped fresh thyme
2 teaspoons chopped fresh basil
1 teaspoon chopped fresh coriander

Combine water and lemon juice in large frying pan, bring to boil, reduce heat, add fish in single layer. Poach over medium heat for about 7 minutes or until just tender. Serve with sauce.

Fresh Herb Sauce: Combine cream and vermouth in small saucepan, bring to boil; reduce heat, simmer for 10 minutes. Add juice, shallots, garlic, capers and herbs. Simmer for 5 minutes or until slightly thickened.

Serves 4.

LEFT: Honey Lime Lobster with Avocado Cream. RIGHT: From top: Salmon Cutlets with Fresh Herb Sauce; Peppered Fish with Lime Butter Sauce.

Plates: Accoutrement

FISH WITH PASSIONFRUIT BEURRE BLANC

We used snapper in this dish. This recipe must be cooked just before serving. Recipe unsuitable to freeze.

6 white fish fillets
1 stick celery, chopped
15g butter
1 bay leaf
PASSIONFRUIT BEURRE BLANC
¼ cup passionfruit pulp
1 tablespoon white vinegar
2 green shallots, chopped
250g butter

Place fish in single layer in large frying pan with celery, butter and bay leaf. Pour in enough water to just cover fish. Bring to boil, reduce heat, simmer, covered, for about 5 minutes (or microwave on HIGH for about 4 minutes) or until fish is just tender; drain on absorbent paper. Serve with passionfruit beurre blanc.

Passionfruit Beurre Blanc: Combine passionfruit pulp, vinegar and shallots in medium saucepan, bring to boil, reduce heat, simmer, uncovered for about 7 minutes or until about 2 tablespoons of the liquid remain. Whisk in cold butter a few pieces at a time. Continue whisking and adding butter over heat until all the butter is used.

Serves 6.

OYSTER AND BACON PARCELS

Filling can be prepared up to several hours ahead; keep, covered, in refrigerator. Parcels are best completed and cooked just before serving. This recipe is not suitable to freeze.

8 sheets fillo pastry
125g butter, melted
¼ cup flaked almonds
OYSTER AND BACON FILLING
3 dozen oysters
⅓ cup dry white wine
⅓ cup water
1 bay leaf
3 black peppercorns
15g butter
3 bacon rashers, chopped
100g mushrooms, chopped
2 tablespoons plain flour
2 tablespoons chopped fresh chives
¼ cup cream

Brush 1 sheet of pastry with melted butter, top with another sheet of pastry, cut in half lengthways. Place 2 tablespoons filling onto end of each strip of pastry. Fold long sides in to cover filling slightly, then roll up from short side. Repeat with remaining pastry and filling.

Place parcels onto lightly greased oven trays, brush with more butter, sprinkle with almonds. Bake in moderately hot oven for about 20 minutes or until golden brown.

Oyster and Bacon Filling: Combine oysters, wine, water, bay leaf and peppercorns in medium saucepan, bring to boil (or microwave on HIGH for about 3 minutes). Remove oysters; strain and reserve liquid.

Melt butter in medium saucepan, add bacon and mushrooms, stir constantly over medium heat for about 3 minutes (or microwave on HIGH for about 2 minutes) or until mushrooms are just tender. Stir in flour, stir over heat further minute (or microwave on HIGH for 1 minute). Remove from heat, gradually stir in reserved liquid, return to heat, stir constantly over high heat (or microwave on HIGH for about 3 minutes) until mixture boils and thickens. Remove from heat, stir in chives, cream and oysters. Cool to room temperature before serving.

Makes 8.

RIGHT: From top: Fish Fillets with Chervil Cream Sauce; Prawn and Camembert Fish Rolls with Lime Sauce. LEFT: From top: Fish with Passionfruit Beurre Blanc; Oyster and Bacon Parcels.

FISH FILLETS WITH CHERVIL CREAM SAUCE

We used John dory in this dish; it is best cooked just before serving. Recipe unsuitable to freeze or microwave.

125g sugar snap peas
4 medium white fish fillets
¾ cup water
2 teaspoons lime juice
1 tablespoon port
1 medium tomato, chopped
300ml carton cream
125g baby mushrooms
3 teaspoons chopped fresh chervil

Top and tail peas. Boil, steam or microwave until just tender; drain. Place fish in single layer in baking dish, add water and juice, cover, bake in moderate oven for about 10 minutes or until almost tender.

Transfer cooking liquid from dish to small saucepan. Cover fish, keep warm in very slow oven. Bring liquid to boil, boil until reduced by half. Add port, tomato and cream. Bring to boil, reduce heat, simmer, uncovered, for about 5 minutes or until mixture is slightly thickened; strain. Return cream mixture to clean saucepan, add peas and mushrooms, cook until peas are heated through. Stir in chervil. Serve sauce with fish.

Serves 4.

PRAWN AND CAMEMBERT FISH ROLLS WITH LIME SAUCE

We used redfish fillets in this recipe. Fish fillets can be rolled with filling and crumbed 2 hours ahead. Lime sauce can be made up to a day ahead. Keep both, covered, in refrigerator. Recipe unsuitable to freeze or microwave.

2 x 125g cans camembert cheese
200g cooked prawns, shelled
8 thin white fish fillets
plain flour
1 egg, lightly beaten
2 tablespoons milk
1 cup packaged breadcrumbs
oil for deep-frying
LIME SAUCE
2 medium limes
15g butter
1 tablespoon chopped fresh chives
2 teaspoons cornflour
¾ cup water
2 teaspoons sugar

Slice camembert thinly. Place prawns and camembert evenly over fish fillets, roll up firmly, secure with toothpicks. Toss rolls lightly in flour, shake off excess flour; dip into combined egg and milk, then coat firmly with breadcrumbs. Deep-fry rolls in hot oil until brown and tender; drain on absorbent paper. Serve with sauce.

Lime Sauce: Remove rind from limes using vegetable peeler; cut rind into fine strips. Squeeze juice from limes; you will need ¼ cup juice for sauce. Melt butter in saucepan, add chives, stir over heat for 1 minute (or microwave on HIGH for 1 minute). Blend cornflour with water, stir into pan with rind, juice and sugar. Stir constantly over high heat (or microwave on HIGH for 3 minutes) or until sauce boils and thickens.

Serves 4.

BALMAIN BUGS IN BRANDY CREAM SAUCE

Prepare recipe just before serving. This recipe is not suitable to freeze.

20 small cooked Balmain bugs
30g butter
1 clove garlic, crushed
200g sugar snap peas
½ teaspoon grated lime rind
2 tablespoons brandy
2 teaspoons cornflour
2 tablespoons water
1 cup cream
2 tablespoons chopped fresh chives

Remove flesh from Balmain bug tails, cut flesh into serving-sized pieces. Heat butter in large frying pan, add garlic, peas and rind, stir constantly over medium heat (or microwave on HIGH for about 2 minutes) until peas are just tender. Add brandy to pan, bring to boil (or microwave on HIGH for about 1 minute). Stir in cornflour blended with water, then cream, chives and Balmain bug flesh. Stir constantly over high heat (or microwave on HIGH for about 3 minutes) or until mixture boils and thickens. Serve with wild rice, if desired.
Serves 4.

SOLE WITH HERB AND PRAWN MOUSSELINE

Fish can be prepared up to 2 hours ahead; cook just before serving. Recipe unsuitable to freeze or microwave.

4 small whole sole
¼ cup lemon juice
¼ cup dry white wine
PRAWN MOUSSELINE
500g uncooked prawns, shelled
1 egg white
¼ cup cream
1 tablespoon chopped fresh dill
2 teaspoons chopped fresh thyme

Trim fins from fish. Cut down backbone to form a pocket on each side of backbone. Spread mousseline into each pocket. Place fish in large baking dish in single layer, sprinkle with lemon juice and wine. Cover, bake in moderate oven for about 20 minutes or until tender.
Prawn Mousseline: Process prawns until minced. Add egg white and cream gradually while motor is operating, stir in herbs.
Serves 4.

LOBSTER THERMIDOR WITH CRUNCHY TOPPING

Prepare recipe as close as possible to serving time. This recipe is not suitable to freeze or microwave.

4 medium uncooked lobster tails
15g butter
1½ tablespoons plain flour
1 cup milk
2 teaspoons prepared German mustard
1 teaspoon seeded mustard
¼ cup cream
CRUNCHY TOPPING
2 tablespoons grated fresh parmesan cheese
½ cup stale breadcrumbs
1 tablespoon chopped fresh chives
½ teaspoon grated lemon rind
15g butter, melted.

Remove flesh from tails, chop flesh into bite-sized pieces. Add lobster shells to large saucepan of boiling water, cook for 1 minute or until shells change colour, drain, rinse under cold water; dry.

Melt butter in small saucepan, stir in flour, stir over medium heat for 1 minute (or microwave on HIGH for 1 minute). Remove from heat, gradually stir in milk, stir constantly over high heat (or microwave on HIGH for about 3 minutes) or until mixture boils and thickens. Stir in mustards and lobster flesh, cook over medium heat for about 2 minutes or until lobster is cooked. Remove from heat; stir in cream. Spoon mixture into lobster shells, sprinkle with topping, grill until lightly browned.
Crunchy Topping: Combine all ingredients in small bowl.
Serves 4.

FISH CUTLETS WITH SPINACH HOLLANDAISE

We used red emperor cutlets in this recipe. Prepare fish and hollandaise as close as possible to serving time for best results. Recipe unsuitable to freeze or microwave.

1 tablespoon oil
30g butter
4 large white fish cutlets
50g roasted macadamia nuts, chopped
SPINACH HOLLANDAISE
½ cup oil
2 cloves garlic, crushed
40 English spinach leaves (or 6 large silverbeet leaves), chopped
2 egg yolks
1 tablespoon lemon juice
1 teaspoon sugar
1 tablespoon French mustard

Heat oil and butter in large frying pan, add fish in single layer, cook for about 3 minutes on each side or until fish is tender; keep warm. Serve with hollandaise, sprinkle with nuts.
Spinach Hollandaise: Heat 1 tablespoon of the oil in medium frying pan, add garlic and spinach, stir over medium heat for about 3 minutes or until spinach is wilted. Blend or process spinach mixture and half the remaining oil until smooth, add egg yolks gradually. Add remaining oil in thin stream while motor is operating; blend until thick and creamy. Stir in juice, sugar and mustard.
Serves 4.

STEAMED WHOLE FISH WITH GINGER SAUCE

We used silver bream in this dish; prepare just before serving. Recipe unsuitable to freeze or microwave.

1 medium carrot
1 stick celery
1 small red pepper
1 small green pepper
4 small whole white fish
1 tablespoon oil
GINGER SAUCE
1 tablespoon grated fresh ginger
2 tablespoons mirin
1 tablespoon light soy sauce
2 tablespoons dry sherry
2 teaspoons cornflour
1 cup water
3 green shallots, chopped

Cut carrot, celery and peppers into thin strips. Boil, steam or microwave until just tender; drain. Fill cavity of each fish with vegetables, secure openings with toothpicks; brush fish lightly with oil. Place fish in large steamer in single layer or on rack in pan over simmering water. Cover, steam for about 10 minutes or until tender. Remove toothpicks, serve with hot sauce.
Ginger Sauce: Combine ginger, mirin, sauce and sherry in small saucepan. Stir in cornflour blended with water, stir over high heat until mixture boils and thickens; add shallots.
Serves 4.

ABOVE: From top: Fish Cutlets with Spinach Hollandaise; Steamed Whole Fish with Ginger Sauce. LEFT: Sole with Herb and Prawn Mousseline. ABOVE LEFT: From top: Lobster Thermidor with Crunchy Topping; Balmain Bug Tails in Brandy Cream Sauce.

OCEAN TROUT WITH WARM CORIANDER VINAIGRETTE

Atlantic salmon can be substituted for trout, if preferred. Vinaigrette can be prepared up to a day ahead; keep, covered, in refrigerator. Fish is best prepared as close to serving time as possible. Recipe unsuitable to freeze.

½ cup water
½ cup dry white wine
¼ cup lemon juice
6 black peppercorns
1 green shallot, chopped
4 ocean trout fillets
1 medium carrot, sliced
1 stick celery, sliced
1 medium zucchini, sliced
1 medium red pepper, sliced
WARM CORIANDER VINAIGRETTE
⅔ cup olive oil
¼ cup dry white wine
1 tablespoon white vinegar
1 clove garlic, crushed
1 teaspoon lemon juice
½ teaspoon grated orange rind
¼ teaspoon French mustard
1 tablespoon chopped fresh coriander

Combine water, wine, juice, peppercorns and shallot in large frying pan, bring to boil, reduce heat. Add fish, cook for 2 minutes. Turn carefully to other side, poach fish for about further 3 minutes (or microwave on HIGH for about 5 minutes) or until tender; drain. Cool slightly before removing skin.

Boil, steam or microwave carrot, celery, zucchini and pepper until just tender; drain. Place on plates, top with fish then vinaigrette.

Warm Coriander Vinaigrette: Whisk oil, wine and vinegar together in small bowl, whisk in remaining ingredients. Heat vinaigrette in small saucepan over low heat until just warm (or microwave on HIGH for about 2 minutes).

Serves 4.

ABOVE: Ocean Trout with Warm Coriander Vinaigrette. RIGHT: Fish Wellington with Mushroom Sauce.

FISH WELLINGTON WITH MUSHROOM SAUCE

Loaf can be cooked a day ahead of wrapping in pastry. We used ling fillets in the loaf. Recipe unsuitable to freeze or microwave.

2 bacon rashers, chopped
1 medium onion, finely chopped
500g white fish fillets, chopped
½ cup stale white breadcrumbs
½ cup cream
2 eggs, separated
1 tablespoon chopped fresh dill
375g packet frozen puff pastry, thawed
MUSHROOM SAUCE
15g butter
1 clove garlic, crushed
1 small onion, finely chopped
250g baby mushrooms, thinly sliced
1 tablespoon brandy
1 teaspoon Worcestershire sauce
1 teaspoon cornflour
¼ cup water
½ large vegetable stock cube, crumbled
½ cup cream

Combine bacon and onion in small frying pan, stir constantly over heat for about 2 minutes (or microwave on HIGH for about 3 minutes) or until onion is soft. Process fish, breadcrumbs, cream, egg whites and dill until combined. Transfer mixture to large bowl, stir in bacon and onion mixture.

Spread into 14cm x 21cm greased loaf pan, bake, uncovered, in moderate oven for about 45 minutes or until firm; cool to room temperature in pan.

Roll pastry to 28cm x 33cm rectangle, brush edges with lightly beaten egg yolks. Place cold fish loaf in centre of pastry, wrap pastry around loaf to enclose completely, press edges together firmly, decorate with scraps of pastry, if desired.

Place loaf onto lightly greased oven tray, brush all over with egg yolks. Bake in moderately hot oven for about 20 minutes or until golden brown, stand 5 minutes before cutting. Serve with mushroom sauce.

Mushroom Sauce: Heat butter in medium frying pan, add garlic and onion, stir constantly over medium heat for 2 minutes (or microwave on HIGH for about 3 minutes) or until onion is soft. Add mushrooms, stir over heat until mushrooms are soft (or microwave on HIGH for 2 minutes). Add brandy and sauce, bring to boil. Blend cornflour with water and stock cube, add to pan with cream, stir constantly over high heat (or microwave on HIGH for about 3 minutes) until sauce boils and thickens.

FISH CUTLETS WITH HAZELNUT HOLLANDAISE

We used barramundi in this dish; prepare fish and hollandaise just before serving. Recipe unsuitable to freeze or microwave.

30g butter
4 medium white fish cutlets
HAZELNUT HOLLANDAISE
¼ cup white vinegar
1 bay leaf
4 fresh parsley stems
125g butter
2 egg yolks
⅓ cup ground packaged hazelnuts

Heat butter in large frying pan, add fish in single layer. Cook over medium heat for about 5 minutes on each side or until fish is lightly browned and tender. Serve with hollandaise.

Hazelnut Hollandaise: Combine vinegar, bay leaf and parsley in small frying pan. Bring to boil, reduce heat, simmer until liquid is reduced to about 2 tablespoons. Strain, reserve liquid; cool. Melt butter in small saucepan. Combine egg yolks, hazelnuts and vinegar mixture in bowl or in top of double saucepan over simmering water. Whisk mixture constantly until thickened. Remove from heat; gradually whisk in hot butter in a thin stream (this should take about 5 minutes), until thickened slightly.

Serves 4.

FISH WITH LEMON SOUFFLE TOPPING AND PIMIENTO COULIS

We used ocean perch fillets in this recipe. Lemon mixture for soufflé topping can be made several hours in advance and left to stand, covered, at room temperature. Before assembling fish and topping, reheat lemon mixture over low heat until just warm, then fold in the beaten egg whites. Coulis can be made up to a day ahead; keep, covered, in refrigerator. Recipe unsuitable to freeze or microwave.

4 medium white fish fillets
30g butter, melted
1 clove garlic, crushed
SOUFFLE TOPPING
30g butter
2 tablespoons plain flour
½ cup milk
2 tablespoons cream
1 teaspoon grated lemon rind
1 tablespoon lemon juice
2 eggs, separated
PIMIENTO COULIS
400g can pimientos, drained
425g can tomatoes
1 teaspoon grated lemon rind
1 teaspoon sugar

Place fish in baking dish in single layer, brush with combined butter and garlic.

Bake in hot oven for 10 minutes (or microwave on HIGH for about 6 minutes) or until tender. Remove fish from oven, drain off excess liquid.

Working quickly, place 2 rounded tablespoons of soufflé topping evenly on each fish fillet. Return fish to hot oven, bake further 10 minutes or until soufflé mixture is puffed and lightly browned. Serve immediately with pimiento coulis.

Soufflé Topping: Heat butter in medium saucepan, add flour, stir over heat for 1 minute (or microwave on HIGH for 1 minute). Remove from heat, gradually stir in combined milk and cream, stir constantly over high heat (or microwave on HIGH for about 2 minutes) until mixture boils and thickens. Remove from heat, stir in rind, juice and egg yolks; transfer mixture to large bowl. Beat egg whites until soft peaks form, fold into lemon mixture.

Pimiento Coulis: Blend or process pimientos and undrained tomatoes until smooth. Strain into small saucepan, add rind and sugar, reheat without boiling.

Serves 4

SEAFOOD PLATTER WITH WARM SALMON DIP

Platter can be prepared several hours ahead of serving; keep, covered, in refrigerator. This recipe is not suitable to freeze or microwave.

500g cooked king prawns
500g mussels
100g broccoli, chopped
½ bunch asparagus
100g sugar snap peas
WARM SALMON DIP
105g can salmon, drained
15g buttter
1 small onion, finely chopped
1 clove garlic, crushed
2 teaspoons plain flour
⅔ cup milk
2 tablespoons grated tasty cheese
2 teaspoons lemon juice
2 teaspoons sour cream
2 teaspoons chopped fresh dill

Shell and devein prawns, leave tails intact. Add mussels gradually in single layer to large saucepan containing about 1 cup of boiling water. Reduce heat, simmer, covered for about 3 minutes or until shells open; remove immediately.

Boil, steam or microwave broccoli, asparagus and peas until just tender; drain, rinse under cold water, drain.

Place seafood and vegetables onto serving plate, serve with dip.

Salmon Dip: Blend or process salmon until smooth. Heat butter in medium saucepan, add onion and garlic, stir over medium heat until onion is soft. Add flour, cook for 1 minute, stirring constantly. Remove from heat, gradually stir in milk, stir constantly over high heat until mixture boils and thickens. Stir in salmon, cheese, juice, cream and dill.

Serves 4.

ABOVE: Seafood Platter with Warm Salmon Dip. ABOVE LEFT: Fish Cutlets with Hazelnut Hollandaise. BELOW LEFT: Fish with Lemon Soufflé Topping and Pimiento Coulis.

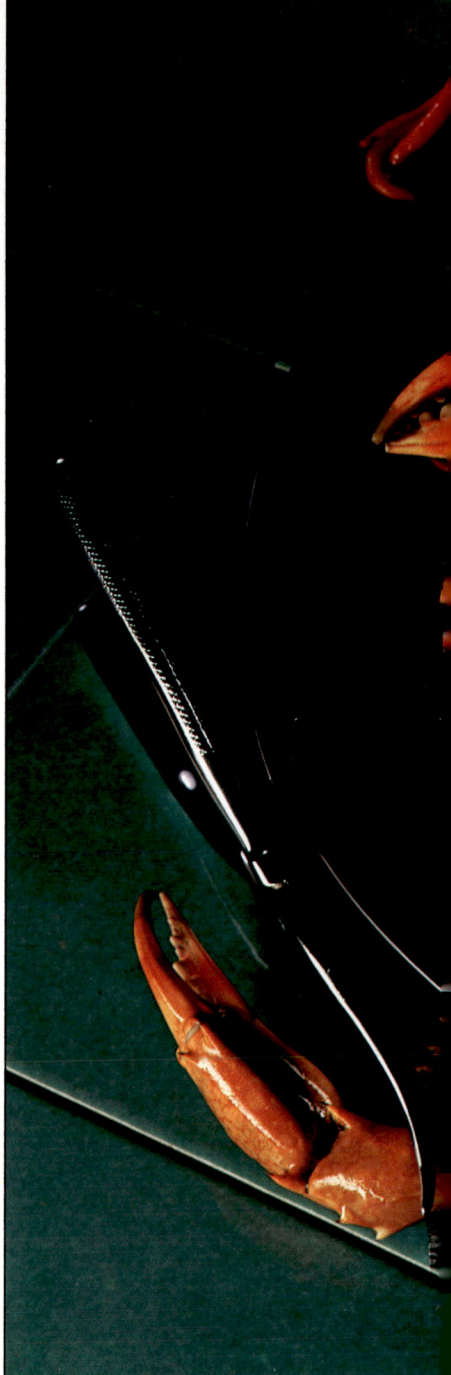

LAMB ROLLS WITH SMOKED SALMON

Lamb can be prepared up to 2 days ahead; keep, covered, in refrigerator, or freeze for up to 2 months. This recipe is not suitable to microwave.

4 large lamb fillets
15g butter, softened
2 teaspoons chopped fresh rosemary
250g sliced smoked salmon
plain flour
2 tablespoons oil
ROSEMARY MINT SAUCE
2 teaspoons plain flour
⅔ cup water
2 teaspoons light soy sauce
2 teaspoons mint sauce
1 teaspoon chopped fresh rosemary

Place lamb between pieces of plastic wrap; flatten lamb with meat mallet. Combine butter and rosemary in small bowl. Place salmon on top of each fillet, spread with butter mixture. Cut in half, roll up from short side like a Swiss roll, secure with toothpicks. Dust rolls lightly with flour, heat oil in large frying pan, add rolls, cook over low heat for about 15 minutes or until tender. Remove from pan, reserve 2 teaspoons pan drippings for sauce. Keep rolls warm while preparing sauce. Serve sliced lamb with sauce.

Rosemary Mint Sauce: Add reserved pan drippings to small saucepan, stir in flour, stir constantly over heat until lightly browned. Remove from heat, gradually stir in water, sauces and rosemary; stir constantly over high heat until mixture boils and thickens.

Serves 4.

CHICKEN AND CRAB WITH AVOCADO SAUCE

Chicken can be prepared up to a day ahead; keep, covered, in refrigerator or freeze for up to 2 months. Sauce must be made just before serving. This recipe is not suitable to microwave.

30g butter
1 small onion, finely chopped
210g can crab, drained
1 tablespoon chopped fresh parsley
4 medium chicken breasts
plain flour
1 tablespoon oil
AVOCADO SAUCE
½ small onion, chopped
2 tablespoons dry white wine
2 tablespoons water
1 tablespoon chopped fresh parsley
½ cup cream
½ cup milk
¼ small avocado
2 teaspoons chopped fresh parsley, extra

Melt butter in small saucepan, add onion, stir constantly over medium heat for about 2 minutes or until onion is soft. Place crab in medium bowl, stir in onion mixture and parsley.

Cut a pocket in underside of each chicken breast, fill with crab mixture. Lightly dust each fillet with flour. Heat oil in medium frying pan, add chicken in single layer, cook on both sides over medium heat for about 15 minutes or until tender. Drain on absorbent paper, serve with warm sauce.

Avocado Sauce: Combine onion,

wine, water and parsley in small saucepan, cook over medium heat until onion is soft and liquid evaporated, add cream and milk, bring to boil, remove from heat, add avocado. Blend or process until combined, stir in extra parsley.

Serves 4.

ABOVE: Sweet Chilli Mud Crabs. LEFT: From top: Chicken and Crab with Avocado Sauce; Lamb Rolls with Smoked Salmon.

SWEET CHILLI MUD CRABS

Crabs are best served immediately they are cooked. This recipe is not suitable to freeze or microwave.

**4 cooked mud crabs
1 teaspoon sesame oil
2 tablespoons oil
2 cloves garlic, finely chopped
2 teaspoons finely chopped fresh ginger
1 small fresh red chilli, finely chopped
¼ cup oyster sauce
¼ cup hoisin sauce
2 tablespoons sweet ground bean sauce
1 cup water
2 teaspoons cornflour
¼ cup water, extra**

Cut crabs in half, crack nippers with nut cracker or mallet. Heat oils in large frying pan or wok, add garlic, ginger and chilli, stir-fry until garlic is lightly browned. Add crabs in 2 batches, stir-fry for 3 minutes; drain.

Return all the crabs to pan, add combined sauces and water; mix well. Cover, cook for 3 minutes. Blend cornflour with extra water, add to pan, stir constantly over high heat until mixture boils and thickens.

Serves 4.

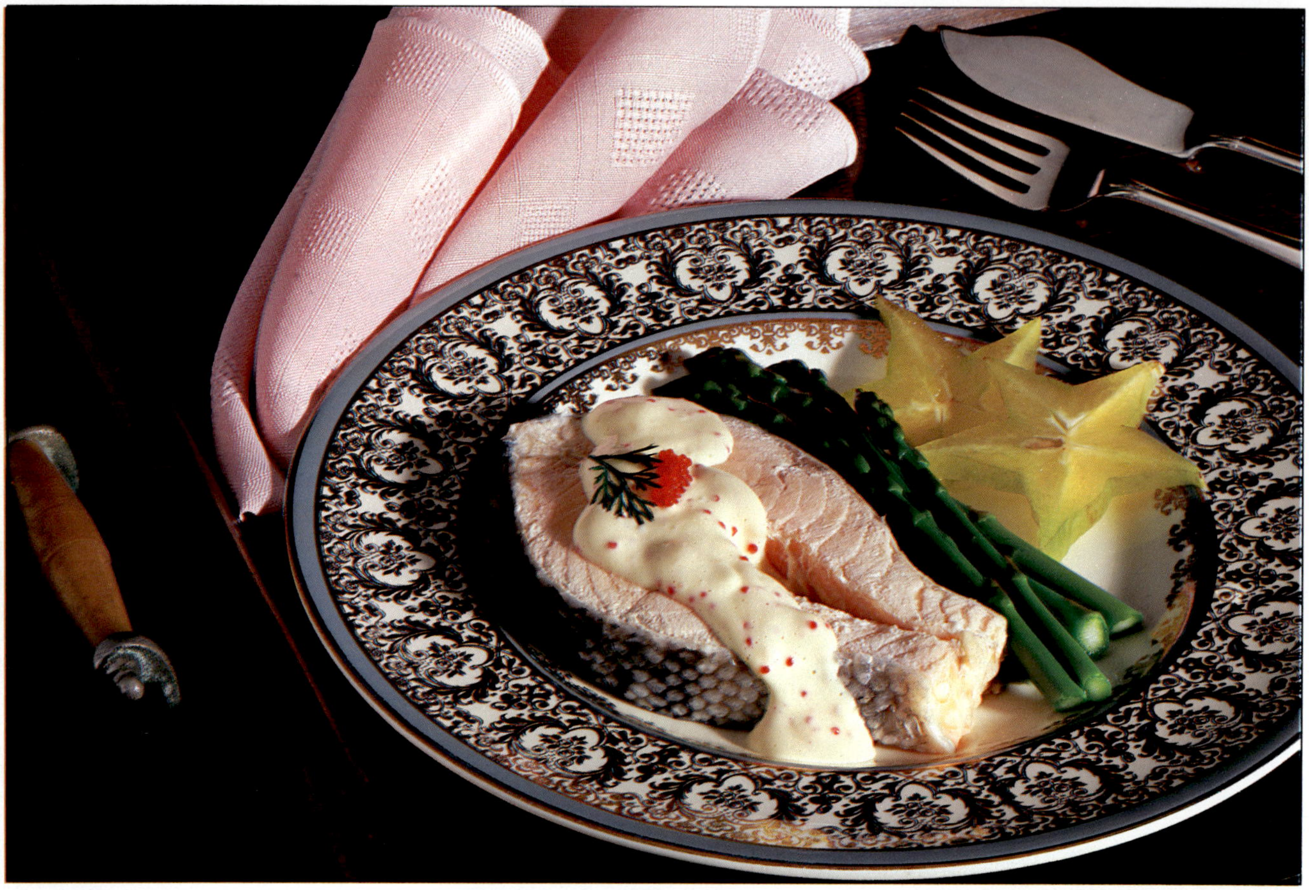

Plate, tray & cutlery: Beecroft Treasure House

SCAMPI WITH CHAMPAGNE SAUCE

Dish is best prepared just before serving. This sauce would also be delicious served over prawns, crabs, marrons, yabbies or lobsters. This recipe is not suitable to freeze or microwave.

1½kg uncooked scampi
30g butter
1 medium leek, sliced
2 tablespoons plain flour
¾ cup champagne
½ cup cream
1 teaspoon sugar
1 tablespoon chopped fresh dill
pinch cayenne pepper

Place scampi in large saucepan, add enough cold water to just cover scampi. Bring to boil, boil for about 5 minutes or until scampi change colour. Drain, reserve 1 cup strained stock. Remove meat from shells in 1 piece, leave tails intact.

Heat butter in medium frying pan, add leek, cook over medium heat for about 5 minutes, stirring occasionally, until leek is soft. Add flour, stir over medium heat for 1 minute, remove from heat. Gradually stir in reserved stock, champagne, cream and sugar, stir constantly over high heat until sauce boils and thickens; stir in dill and pepper. Serve with warm scampi.

Serves 4.

Plate: Dansab

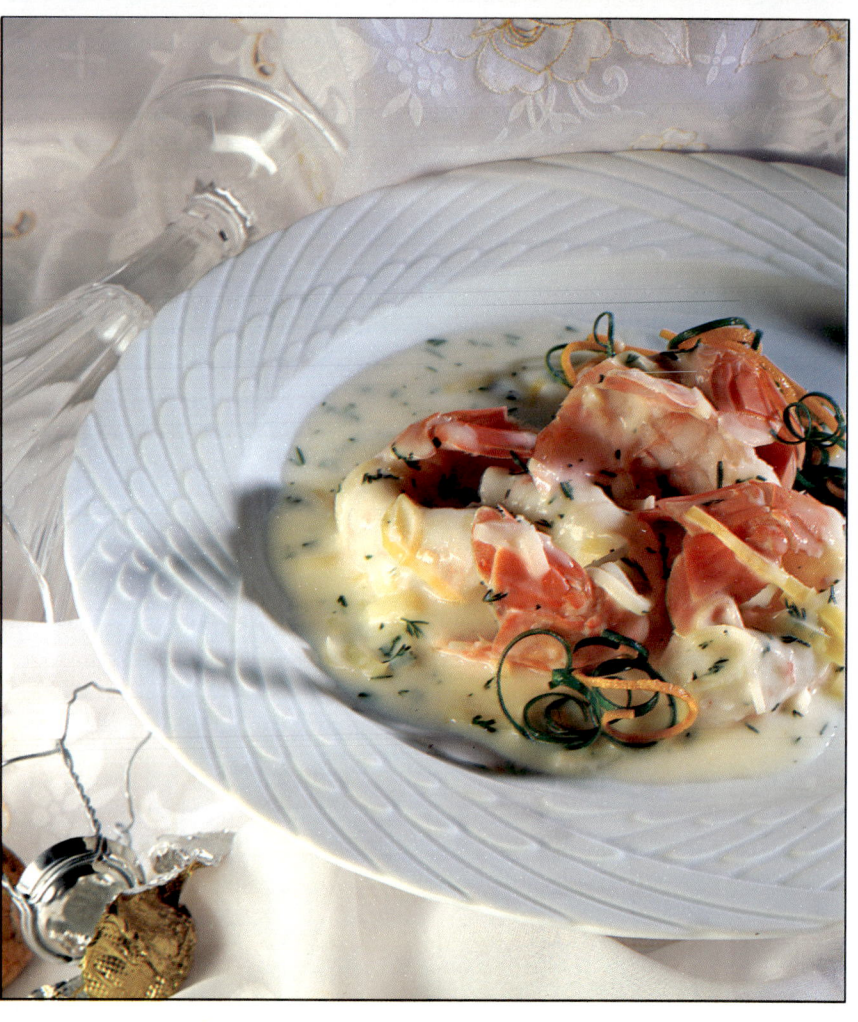

POACHED SALMON WITH CAVIAR HOLLANDAISE

Ocean trout can be substituted for salmon in this recipe, if desired. Recipe unsuitable to freeze or microwave.

4 medium Atlantic salmon steaks
2 sprigs dill
2 small onions, sliced
6 black peppercorns
CAVIAR HOLLANDAISE
½ cup white tarragon vinegar
6 black peppercorns
1 bay leaf
4 egg yolks
250g butter
1 teaspoon lemon juice
50g jar red lumpfish caviar

Place steaks in single layer in large frying pan, cover with water, add dill, onions and peppercorns. Bring to boil, reduce heat, simmer, uncovered, for about 8 minutes or until tender. Lift fish carefully onto plates, serve with caviar hollandaise.

Caviar Hollandaise: Combine vinegar, peppercorns and bay leaf in medium saucepan, bring to boil, reduce heat, simmer, uncovered, until liquid is reduced to about half; strain, cool.

Blend or process egg yolks until combined, gradually add hot bubbly butter in a thin stream while motor is operating, blend until mixture begins to thicken.

Add about 2 teaspoons of the cold vinegar mixture to blender, then add more melted butter. When mixture begins to thicken again, add another 2 teaspoons vinegar. Continue in this way until all butter and vinegar have been used. Stir in juice and caviar.

Serves 4.

ABOVE: Pork and Prawn Paupiettes with Blue Cheese Sauce. LEFT: Scampi with Champagne Sauce. ABOVE LEFT: Poached Salmon with Caviar Hollandaise.

PORK AND PRAWN PAUPIETTES WITH BLUE CHEESE SAUCE

Paupiettes can be made a day ahead or frozen for 2 months. Recipe unsuitable to microwave.

12 English spinach leaves
4 large pork schnitzels
8 cooked king prawns, shelled
plain flour
2 tablespoons oil
BLUE CHEESE SAUCE
2 teaspoons butter
2 teaspoons plain flour
½ cup water
¼ large vegetable stock cube, crumbled
¼ cup cream
30g soft blue cheese
2 teaspoons chopped fresh parsley

Boil, steam or microwave spinach until just wilted; rinse in cold water, drain well. (You can use pieces of spinach (silverbeet) leaves instead of English spinach; cut them into pieces large enough to cover the pork, if desired.) Pound schnitzels until thin, divide spinach evenly between schnitzels, cut prawns in half lengthways, place on top of spinach. Roll up to enclose prawns, secure with toothpicks. Dust rolls lightly in flour; shake off excess flour. Heat oil in medium frying pan, add paupiettes, cook gently for about 20 minutes or until tender. Remove toothpicks, serve with sauce.

Blue Cheese Sauce: Melt butter in small saucepan, add flour, stir over medium heat for 1 minute (or microwave on HIGH for about 30 seconds). Remove from heat, gradually stir in water, stock cube, cream and cheese. Return to heat, stir constantly over high heat (or microwave on HIGH for about 2 minutes) until mixture boils and thickens. Stir in parsley.

Serves 4.

FAMILY MAIN MEALS

The meal appeal of seafood is boundless, and in this section you will find tasty recipes that will satisfy your family's appetites yet be easy and quick (some unbelievably quick) to prepare. Many are complete meals in themselves and you won't need to cook extra vegetables unless you specially want them.

SEAFOOD AND BACON PIZZA

You will need to cook 1kg mussels for this recipe. Wholemeal self-raising flour can be substituted for white flour, if preferred. Pizza is best made just before serving. This recipe is not suitable to freeze or microwave.

4 bacon rashers, chopped
¼ cup tomato sauce
1 medium onion, finely chopped
250g cooked mussel meat, chopped
375g uncooked prawns, shelled, chopped
1 medium green pepper, chopped
2 cups (250g) grated mozzarella cheese
½ teaspoon dried oregano leaves
SCONE DOUGH
1 cup self-raising flour
15g butter
⅓ cup milk, approximately

Cook bacon in frying pan until crisp, drain on absorbent paper (or microwave on HIGH for about 3 minutes).

Roll out dough large enough to fit greased 28cm pizza pan. Spread dough with sauce, top with onion, mussels, prawns, pepper, bacon, cheese and oregano. Bake in hot oven for about 15 minutes or until brown.

Scone Dough: Sift flour into medium bowl, rub in butter, add enough milk to mix to a firm dough. Turn onto lightly floured surface, knead until smooth.

LEFT: Seafood and Bacon Pizza.
RIGHT: Fish and Rice Puff.

FISH AND RICE PUFF

Filling for puff can be made up to 3 days ahead; keep, covered, in refrigerator. You will need to cook about ¼ cup rice for this recipe. Assemble fish just before baking; serve as soon as it is cooked. Recipe unsuitable to freeze or microwave.

½ cup peas
1 small carrot, finely chopped
¾ cup cooked rice
1 small onion, finely chopped
1 egg, lightly beaten
1 tablespoon chopped fresh parsley
440g can salmon, drained
2 sheets ready-rolled puff pastry
1 egg yolk
1 tablespoon milk

Boil, steam or microwave peas and carrot until tender, drain. Combine peas and carrot with rice, onion, egg, parsley and salmon in medium bowl. Cut pastry sheets into large fish shapes; cut 1 about 1cm larger all round than the other.

Place smaller shape onto greased oven tray, top evenly with fish mixture, leaving 1cm border. Brush border with combined egg yolk and milk. Top fish with remaining pastry, press edges together firmly. Make fins and tail from pastry scraps, attach to fish.

Brush fish all over with egg mixture, bake in hot oven for about 25 minutes. Cover fins and tail with foil during baking, if necessary, to prevent them from burning. Reduce heat to moderate, bake further 20 minutes or until well browned.

Serves 4.

CURRIED PRAWN AND VEGETABLE STIR-FRY

Cook stir-fry as close as possible to serving time. This recipe is not suitable to freeze or microwave.

**500g uncooked prawns
2 teaspoons oil
¼ teaspoon sesame oil
1 clove garlic, crushed
1 teaspoon curry powder
½ x 425g can baby corn, drained
1 medium carrot, chopped
1 teaspoon cornflour
½ cup water
½ small chicken stock cube, crumbled
2 teaspoons light soy sauce
2 green shallots, chopped**

Shell and devein prawns, leaving tails intact. Heat oils in wok or large frying pan, add garlic and curry powder, stir-fry over heat for about 30 seconds. Add prawns, stir-fry over high heat until prawns are almost cooked. Add corn and carrot, stir-fry for 1 minute. Stir in cornflour blended with water, stock cube and sauce. Add to pan, stir constantly over high heat until mixture boils and thickens; add shallots.

Serves 2.

CRISPY FISH BALLS IN BLACK BEAN SAUCE

We used ling fillets in this recipe. Fish balls can be crumbed, ready for cooking, several hours ahead; keep, covered, in refrigerator. This recipe is not suitable to freeze or microwave.

**500g white fish fillets, chopped
4 green shallots, chopped
½ teaspoon grated fresh ginger
1 clove garlic, crushed
1 egg, lightly beaten
½ cup stale breadcrumbs
2 teaspoons lemon juice
¼ cup plain flour
1 egg, lightly beaten, extra
1 tablespoon milk
1 cup packaged breadcrumbs
2 tablespoons oil
1 medium onion, quartered
1 medium red pepper, thinly sliced
1 medium green pepper, thinly sliced
1 tablespoon dry sherry
¼ cup sweet ground bean sauce
1 tablespoon lemon juice, extra
1¼ cups water**

Process fish, shallots, ginger, garlic, egg, stale breadcrumbs and lemon juice until combined. Transfer mixture to medium bowl, cover, refrigerate for about 30 minutes or until mixture is firm enough to handle.

Shape heaped tablespoons of mixture into balls, roll in flour, refrigerate balls for 30 minutes. Dip balls into combined extra egg and milk, then toss in packaged breadcrumbs. Heat oil in large frying pan, add fish balls, cook over medium heat for about 15 minutes or until golden brown; drain on absorbent paper.

Add onion and peppers to pan, stir constantly over medium heat for about 2 minutes or until onion is just soft. Add sherry, bean sauce, extra juice and water; bring to boil. Add fish balls, reduce heat, simmer, uncovered, for about 3 minutes, or until heated through. Serve with boiled rice.

Serves 4.

BELOW: From left: Crispy Fish Balls in Black Bean Sauce; Curried Prawn and Vegetable Stir-Fry. RIGHT: From top: Fish and Potato Loaf with Fresh Tomato Sauce; Fish Patties with Lemon and Chive Mayonnaise.

FISH AND POTATO LOAF WITH FRESH TOMATO SAUCE

You can use any fish of your choice in this recipe. Atlantic salmon can be substituted for ocean trout. Recipe is best served immediately it is made. Recipe unsuitable to freeze.

1 small flat Vienna loaf
1 medium potato
2 ocean trout fillets
3 green shallots, chopped
1 teaspoon chopped fresh dill
¼ cup cream
1 egg
FRESH TOMATO SAUCE
15g butter
1 clove garlic, crushed
1 small onion, chopped
3 ripe tomatoes, peeled, chopped
½ cup water
½ cup dry white wine
1 teaspoon sugar
½ large vegetable stock cube, crumbled

Cut one-third from top of bread. Remove crumbs from inside of loaf, leaving crust 1cm thick. Reserve crumbs for future use.

Cut potato into 1cm cubes; boil, steam or microwave until tender, cool. Poach fish in frying pan of simmering water for about 3 minutes (or microwave on MEDIUM HIGH for about 5 minutes) or until tender; drain, flake.

Combine fish, potato, shallots and dill in large bowl, spoon into hollow loaf. Pour in combined cream and egg. Replace top of loaf, wrap loaf securely in foil, place on oven tray. Bake in moderately hot oven for about 45 minutes or until filling is just set. Serve with sauce.

Fresh Tomato Sauce: Heat butter in small frying pan, add garlic and onion, stir over medium heat for about 2 minutes (or microwave on high for about 3 minutes) or until onion is soft. Add tomatoes, water, wine, sugar and stock cube, bring to boil, reduce heat (or microwave on HIGH for about 3 minutes). Simmer, uncooked, for about 10 minutes (or microwave on HIGH for about 5 minutes) or until tomatoes are soft. Blend or process sauce until well combined.

Serves 4 to 6.

FISH PATTIES WITH LEMON AND CHIVE MAYONNAISE

We used ling fillets in this recipe. Patties can be prepared ready for cooking a day ahead; keep, covered, in refrigerator. This recipe is not suitable to freeze or microwave.

750g white fish fillets, chopped
1 cup stale breadcrumbs
2 tablespoons chopped fresh chives
1 tablespoon chopped fresh mint
1 tablespoon lemon juice
2 tablespoons fruit chutney
plain flour
15g butter
2 tablespoons oil
LEMON AND CHIVE MAYONNAISE
2 tablespoons lemon juice
2 tablespoons chopped fresh chives
½ cup mayonnaise

Blend or process fish until smooth, transfer mixture to large bowl. Mix in breadcrumbs, chives, mint, juice and chutney. Divide mixture into 8 portions, shape into patties; toss in flour.

Heat butter and oil in large frying pan. Add patties, cook over medium heat for about 20 minutes or until cooked through. Drain on absorbent paper, serve with mayonnaise.

Lemon and Chive Mayonnaise: Combine all ingredients in small bowl.

Makes 8.

CURRIED PRAWNS AND VEGETABLES

Curry is best made just before serving, or it can be frozen for up to 2 months.

2 tablespoons oil
1 medium onion, chopped
1 medium carrot, chopped
1 stick celery, chopped
¼ cup sultanas
2 teaspoons curry powder
1½ tablespoons plain flour
1 tablespoon coconut
1½ cups water
½ large vegetable stock cube, crumbled
500g shelled uncooked prawns
½ cup frozen green peas

Heat oil in medium saucepan, add onion, carrot and celery. Stir constantly over medium heat for 2 minutes (or microwave on HIGH for about 3 minutes). Add sultanas, curry powder, flour and coconut, stir constantly over medium heat for 1 minute (or microwave on HIGH for about 30 seconds).

Remove from heat, gradually stir in water and stock cube, stir constantly over high heat (or microwave on HIGH for about 5 minutes) or until mixture boils and thickens. Add prawns and peas, stir constantly over medium heat for 2 minutes (or microwave on HIGH for about 4 minutes) or until prawns are tender.
Serves 4.

ABOVE: From left: Fish Florentine; Curried Prawns and Vegetables. RIGHT: From top: Minted Apricot Fish; Curried Smoked Fish Pasties.

FISH FLORENTINE

We used ling fillets in this recipe. The dish can be prepared up to the stage of cooking several hours ahead, keep, covered, in refrigerator. This recipe is not suitable to freeze.

30g butter
1 clove garlic, crushed
4 large spinach (silverbeet) leaves, chopped
500g white fish fillets
30g butter, extra
2 tablespoons plain flour
¾ cup milk
½ cup cream
½ cup grated tasty cheese
1 teaspoon grated lemon rind
2 tablespoons grated parmesan cheese

Melt butter in frying pan, add garlic and spinach, stir constantly over heat for about 2 minutes (or microwave on HIGH for about 3 minutes) or until spinach is tender. Spread spinach into shallow ovenproof dish (6 cup capacity). Poach, steam or microwave fish until tender, chop roughly, spread evenly over spinach.

Melt extra butter in medium saucepan, add flour, stir over heat further minute (or microwave on HIGH for 1 minute). Remove from heat, gradually stir in combined milk and cream, return to heat, stir constantly over high heat (or microwave on HIGH for about 3 minutes) or until mixture boils and thickens.

Stir in tasty cheese and rind, spread over fish, sprinkle with parmesan cheese. Bake in moderate oven for about 20 minutes (or microwave on HIGH for about 5 minutes) or until hot.
Serves 4.

MINTED APRICOT FISH

We used ocean perch fillets in this recipe. Fish can be marinated in apricot mixture for several hours; keep, covered, in refrigerator. This recipe is not suitable to freeze.

6 large white fish fillets
425g can apricot nectar
30g packet French onion soup mix
1 tablespoon lemon juice
2 tablespoons chopped fresh mint

Place fish into baking dish in single layer. Combine remaining ingredients in small bowl, pour over fish. Cover, bake in moderate oven for about 45 minutes (or microwave on HIGH for about 7 minutes) or until fish is tender.
Serves 6.

CURRIED SMOKED FISH PASTIES

We used smoked cod in this recipe. Filling can be prepared a day ahead. Cook completed pasties as close to serving time as possible. Cooked pasties can be frozen for 2 months. This recipe unsuitable to microwave.

60g butter
1 medium potato, finely chopped
1 medium carrot, finely chopped
1 medium onion, finely chopped
500g smoked fish, chopped
2 teaspoons curry powder
2 tablespoons plain flour
1 cup milk
1 tablespoon lemon juice
¼ cup frozen peas
2 teaspoons brown sugar
5 sheets ready-rolled puff pastry
1 egg, lightly beaten
1 tablespoon sesame seeds

Heat butter in medium saucepan, add potato, carrot and onion. Stir constantly over medium heat for about 2 minutes (or microwave on HIGH for 3 minutes) or until onion is soft. Stir in fish, curry powder and flour, stir constantly over medium heat for 1 minute (or microwave on HIGH for 1 minute). Remove from heat, gradually stir in milk, return to heat, stir constantly over high heat (or microwave on HIGH for about 3 minutes) until mixture boils and thickens. Stir in juice, peas and sugar; cool to room temperature.

Cut 10cm circles from pastry sheets, brush edges with egg. Place a level tablespoon of mixture into centre of each circle, fold over to enclose filling, roll and fold edges, as pictured. Place pasties onto lightly greased oven trays, brush lightly with egg, sprinkle with sesame seeds. Bake in moderately hot oven for about 25 minutes or until golden brown.
Makes about 20.

TUNA AND SPINACH BAKE

This dish is best prepared just before cooking. This recipe is not suitable to freeze or microwave.

30g butter
1 medium onion, chopped
6 large spinach (silverbeet) leaves, chopped
425g can tuna, drained, flaked
¾ cup evaporated milk
3 eggs, lightly beaten
¾ cup grated tasty cheese
½ cup packaged breadcrumbs

Melt butter in medium frying pan, add onion, stir over heat for about 2 minutes or until onion is soft. Add spinach to pan, cover, cook for about 2 minutes or until wilted; drain well. Spread spinach mixture into ovenproof dish (6 cup capacity). Top with tuna, then combined milk and eggs. Sprinkle evenly with combined cheese and breadcrumbs. Bake in moderate oven for about 40 minutes or until heated through and golden brown.
   Serves 4.

CRUMBED FISH WITH TOMATO ONION SAUCE

We used thick ling fillets in this recipe. Fish is best cooked as close to serving time as possible. Sauce can be made up to a day ahead; keep, covered, in refrigerator. This recipe is not suitable to freeze.

500g white fish fillets
plain flour
1 egg, lightly beaten
2 tablespoons milk
1 cup packaged breadcrumbs
¼ cup grated parmesan cheese
oil for deep-frying
TOMATO ONION SAUCE
1 tablespoon oil
1 medium onion, finely chopped
310g can Tomato Supreme
2 tablespoons tomato sauce
¼ cup water
1 teaspoon sugar
1 tablespoon chopped fresh parsley

Cut fish into strips, toss in flour. Dip fish into combined egg and milk, then combined breadcrumbs and cheese. Deep-fry fish in hot oil until golden brown, drain on absorbent paper, serve with sauce.

Tomato Onion Sauce: Heat oil in small saucepan, add onion, stir over heat for about 2 minutes (or microwave on HIGH for about 3 minutes) or until onion is soft. Add Tomato Supreme, sauce, water and sugar. Bring to boil, reduce heat, simmer, uncovered, for 2 minutes (or microwave on HIGH for 3 minutes). Stir in parsley.
   Serves 4.

BELOW: Tuna and Spinach Bake. RIGHT: From top: Smoked Fish Ring; Crumbed Fish with Tomato Onion Sauce.

SMOKED FISH RING

We used smoked haddock in this recipe. Filling can be prepared several hours ahead; keep, covered, in refrigerator. This recipe is not suitable to freeze or microwave.

30g butter
1 medium onion, finely chopped
1 tablespoon seeded mustard
375g smoked fish, chopped
250g baby mushrooms, sliced
3 green shallots, chopped
CHEESE SAUCE
30g butter
2 tablespoons plain flour
1½ cups milk
½ cup grated tasty cheese
CHOUX RING
1 cup water
75g butter, chopped
1 cup plain flour
4 eggs, lightly beaten

Heat butter in large frying pan, add onion, stir over medium heat for about 2 minutes (or microwave on HIGH for about 3 minutes) or until onion is soft. Stir in mustard, fish and mushrooms. Stir over heat 1 minute, stir in cheese sauce and shallots.

Place lower half of choux ring onto oven tray, fill with fish mixture, cover with top half of choux ring. Bake in moderate oven for about 10 minutes or until heated through.

Cheese Sauce: Melt butter in small saucepan, stir in flour, stir over heat for 1 minute (or microwave on HIGH for 2 minutes). Remove from heat, gradually stir in milk, return to heat, stir constantly over high heat (or microwave on HIGH for about 3 minutes) or until mixture boils and thickens. Add cheese, stir until melted and smooth.

Choux Ring: Grease oven tray, mark 23cm circle on tray. Combine water and butter in medium saucepan. Bring to boil, stirring, until butter is melted.

Add flour all at once. Stir vigorously over medium heat with wooden spoon until mixture leaves side of pan and forms a smooth ball. Place in small bowl of electric mixer (or in processor). Add eggs gradually, beating well on low speed after each addition.

Place mixture in large piping bag without a tube, pipe around marked circle on tray. Bake in hot oven for 12 minutes, reduce heat, bake in moderate oven further 20 minutes or until browned and well puffed. Prick all over with skewer to release steam. Return to moderate oven for 10 minutes; cool. Split pastry ring in half, scoop out doughy centre, return to moderate oven for about 3 minutes or until ring is dry and crisp.

Serves 6.

CRUNCHY POTATO-TOPPED TUNA BAKE

Tuna mixture can be prepared up to a day ahead; keep, covered, in refrigerator. Spread with topping just before baking. This recipe is not suitable to freeze.

1 tablespoon oil
1 medium onion, sliced
1 clove garlic, crushed
1 medium red pepper, chopped
2 sticks celery, chopped
425g can tomatoes
¼ teaspoon tabasco sauce
½ teaspoon sugar
3 teaspoons cornflour
⅓ cup water
2 tablespoons chopped fresh basil
425g can tuna in brine, drained
paprika
POTATO TOPPING
2 medium potatoes
¾ cup grated tasty cheese
30g butter, melted

Heat oil in large frying pan, add onion and garlic, sir constantly over medium heat for about 2 minutes (or microwave on HIGH for about 3 minutes) or until onion is soft. Add pepper and celery to pan, stir constantly over heat for 2 minutes (or microwave on HIGH for 2 minutes). Stir in undrained crushed tomatoes, tabasco and sugar, bring to boil, remove from heat.

Blend cornflour with water, add to tomato mixture, stir constantly over high heat (or microwave on HIGH for about 3 minutes) or until mixture boils and thickens. Stir in basil and flaked tuna. Spread mixture into shallow ovenproof dish (7 cup capacity). Spread evenly with topping, sprinkle with paprika, bake in moderately hot oven for about 30 minutes or until topping is crisp and golden brown.

Potato Topping: Grate potatoes coarsely, squeeze as much liquid as possible from potato with hand. Combine potatoes, cheese and butter in medium bowl, mix well.

Serves 4.

CREAMY FISH AND POTATO BAKE

We used whiting fillets in this dish. Recipe can be prepared up to a day ahead; keep, covered, in refrigerator. This recipe is not suitable to freeze or microwave.

375g white fish fillets
3 large old potatoes, thinly sliced
1 egg, lightly beaten
300ml carton cream
¼ teaspoon ground nutmeg
1 cup grated tasty cheese

Poach fish in simmering water for about 3 minutes or until tender; drain, flake. Place half the potatoes in greased 17cm x 30cm ovenproof dish, sprinkle with fish, top with remaining potatoes. Combine egg, cream and nutmeg, pour into dish, sprinkle with cheese. Bake in moderate oven for about 40 minutes or until lightly browned; stand for 5 minutes.

Serves 4.

WHOLE FISH WITH MUSTARD GLAZE

We used trevally in this recipe. Prepare fish just before serving. This recipe is not suitable to freeze.

4 small whole white fish
plain flour
30g butter
SPRING VEGETABLE MIX
1 small carrot
1 small zucchini
1 bunch (40 leaves) English spinach, chopped
MUSTARD GLAZE
15g butter
1 small onion, finely chopped
1 cup water
½ large vegetable stock cube, crumbled
1 teaspoon seeded mustard
2 teaspoons cornflour
1 tablespoon water, extra
1 tablespoon chopped fresh chives

Lightly dust fish with flour. Heat butter in large frying pan, add fish in single layer. Cook over medium heat for about 5 minutes on each side or until fish are tender. Serve fish on vegetables, top with sauce.

Spring Vegetable Mix: Cut carrot and zucchini into thin strips. Boil, steam or microwave vegetables until just tender; drain.

Mustard Glaze: Heat butter in small saucepan, add onion, stir constantly over medium heat for about 2 minutes (or microwave on HIGH for about 3 minutes) or until onion is soft. Add water, stock cube and mustard, bring to boil. Stir in cornflour blended with extra water, stir constantly over high heat (or microwave on HIGH for about 2 minutes) or until sauce boils and thickens; add chives.

Serves 4.

Clockwise from left: Crunchy Potato Topped Tuna Bake; Creamy Fish and Potato Bake: Whole Fish with Mustard Glaze.

Casserole dishes: Kitchen Collection; ship in bottle & cutlery: Beecroft Treasure House

CRUNCHY-TOPPED SMOKED FISH WITH BROCCOLI

We used smoked cod in this dish. Recipe can be prepared a day before required; keep covered, in refrigerator. This recipe is not suitable to freeze.

500g smoked fish
750g broccoli, chopped
500g cauliflower, chopped
45g butter
¼ cup plain flour
2 cups milk
¼ cup grated tasty cheese
1 tablespoon grated parmesan cheese
½ cup stale breadcrumbs
½ cup grated tasty cheese, extra
15g butter, melted, extra

Add fish to frying pan of cold water, cover, bring to boil; drain. Repeat this process. Cool fish, chop coarsely. Boil, steam or microwave broccoli and cauliflower until tender; drain.

Melt butter in medium saucepan, add flour, stir constantly over heat for 1 minute (or microwave on HIGH for 1 minute), remove from heat. Gradually stir in milk, return to heat, stir constantly over high heat (or microwave on HIGH for about 3 minutes), or until mixture boils and thickens. Remove from heat, add cheeses, stir until melted.

Spread half sauce mixture into ovenproof dish (5 cup capacity). Top with fish, broccoli and cauliflower, then remaining sauce. Sprinkle with combined breadcrumbs, extra cheese and extra butter. Bake in moderate oven for about 25 minutes or until golden brown.

Serves 4.

SEAFOOD FRIED RICE

We used gemfish in this recipe. Recipe can be made up to a day ahead; keep, covered, in refrigerator. This recipe is not suitable to freeze or microwave.

¾ cup brown rice
¾ cup white rice
2 eggs
1 teaspoon sesame oil
1 tablespoon oil
250g scallops
200g white fish fillets, chopped
½ teaspoon ground ginger
¼ teaspoon ground coriander
1 tablespoon brown sugar
8 green shallots, chopped
1 medium red pepper, chopped
1 stick celery, chopped
½ × 425g can baby corn, sliced
500g cooked prawns, shelled
1 tablespoon light soy sauce
2 tablespoons chopped fresh coriander

Add brown rice gradually to large saucepan of boiling water, boil rapidly, uncovered, for 15 minutes. Add white rice, boil further 10 minutes or until both are tender. Drain, rinse under cold water, drain well.

Spread rice out on large oven trays, bake in moderate oven for about 20 minutes or until rice is dry, stir every 5 minutes; cool to room temperature.

Beat eggs in small bowl with sesame oil. Heat oil in wok or frying pan, pour egg mixture into pan to make omelette, cook until base is lightly browned. Turn, cook other side, remove from pan. Roll up omelette, cut into thin strips.

Add scallops and fish to pan, stir-fry for a few minutes over medium heat or until fish is cooked. Add spices, sugar, shallots, pepper, celery, corn, rice, omelette strips and prawns, stir-fry for a few minutes. Add sauce and coriander.

Serves 4.

BELOW: From top: Crunchy-Topped Smoked Fish with Broccoli; Seafood Fried Rice. RIGHT: From top: Fish and Vegetable Hot Pot; Fish Cottage Pie.

FISH COTTAGE PIE

We used gemfish fillets in this recipe. Pie can be made up to 2 days ahead; keep, covered, in refrigerator. This recipe is not suitable to freeze.

2 medium potatoes, chopped
200g pumpkin, chopped
2 tablespoons milk
15g butter
1 medium onion, chopped
2 cups frozen mixed vegetables, thawed
½ cup milk, extra
½ large vegetable stock cube, crumbled
2 tablespoons plain flour
¼ cup water
600g white fish fillets, coarsely chopped
2 tablespoons grated parmesan cheese

Boil, steam or microwave potatoes and pumpkin until tender, drain. Add milk, mash until smooth.

Melt butter in large frying pan, add onion, stir constantly over heat for about 2 minutes (or microwave on HIGH for about 3 minutes) or until onion is soft. Add vegetables, extra milk, stock cube and flour blended with water. Stir over high heat (or microwave on HIGH for about 4 minutes) until mixture boils and thickens.

Add fish, mix lightly, pour into ovenproof dish (5 cup capacity), top with mashed potato mixture, sprinkle with cheese. Bake in moderate oven for about 30 minutes or until brown.

Serves 4.

FISH AND VEGETABLE HOT POT

We used gemfish fillets in this recipe. The dish can be prepared several hours ahead of serving. This recipe is not suitable to freeze.

125g broccoli, chopped
3 small zucchini, sliced
30g butter
1 small onion, finely chopped
1 clove garlic, crushed
¼ cup plain flour
2 cups water
1 small chicken stock cube, crumbled
750g white fish fillets, coarsely chopped
¼ cup dry white wine
2 tablespoons cream
440g can potatoes, drained, halved
125g frozen baby carrots, thawed
¼ cup chopped fresh parsley

Boil, steam or microwave broccoli and zucchini until just tender; drain. Melt butter in large saucepan, add onion and garlic, stir constantly over medium heat for about 2 minutes (or microwave on HIGH for about 3 minutes) or until onion is soft. Add flour, cook for 1 minute, stirring constantly.

Remove from heat, gradually stir in water and stock cube, stir constantly over high heat (or microwave on HIGH for about 3 minutes) until sauce boils and thickens. Add fish, wine, cream, potatoes and carrots.

Cook over medium heat for about 5 minutes (or microwave on HIGH for about 3 minutes) or until fish is tender. Gently mix in broccoli, zucchini and parsley, cook over low heat (or microwave on HIGH for about 3 minutes) or until heated through.

Serves 4.

CRUNCHY-TOPPED PRAWN AND ASPARAGUS BAKE

This dish can be made several hours ahead; keep, covered, in refrigerator. Bake just before required. Prawn and asparagus mixture can be frozen for up to 2 months.

30g butter
1 clove garlic, crushed
2 sticks celery, chopped
1 medium red pepper, chopped
500g uncooked prawns, shelled, chopped
2 tablespoons plain flour
1¼ cups milk
440g can asparagus pieces, drained
1 cup grated tasty cheese
1½ cups stale white breadcrumbs
60g butter, melted, extra

Melt butter in medium saucepan, add garlic, celery, pepper and prawns. Stir constantly over medium heat (or microwave on HIGH for about 3 minutes) or until prawns are tender. Add flour, stir over heat further minute, remove from heat, gradually stir in milk. Return to heat, stir constantly over heat (or microwave on HIGH for about 3 minutes) or until mixture boils and thickens. Remove from heat, stir in asparagus and half the cheese. Spoon mixture into shallow ovenproof dish (6 cup capacity).

Combine remaining cheese, breadcrumbs and extra butter in bowl; sprinkle over prawn mixture. Bake in moderately hot oven for about 20 minutes or until golden brown. Serve with boiled rice, if desired.

Serves 4.

LAYERED EGGPLANT AND FISH CASSEROLE

We used gemfish fillets in this recipe. Casserole can be made up to 3 days ahead; keep, covered, in refrigerator. This recipe is not suitable to freeze.

2 small eggplants, thickly sliced
1 tablespoon salt
½ cup oil
plain flour
2 tablespoons oil, extra
1 medium onion, finely chopped
425g can tomatoes, drained
2 tablespoons tomato paste
500g white fish fillets, finely chopped
½ cup grated tasty cheese

CHEESE SAUCE
45g butter
¼ cup plain flour
1¾ cups milk
½ cup grated tasty cheese

Place eggplants in bowl, sprinkle with salt, stand for 15 minutes. Rinse eggplants well under cold water, drain, dry on absorbent paper.

Heat half the oil in large frying pan. Lightly dust half the eggplants with flour, add to pan, fry until lightly browned on both sides; drain on absorbent paper. Repeat with remaining oil and eggplants.

Heat extra oil in medium saucepan, add onion, cook over medium heat for about 2 minutes or until onion is soft. Add crushed tomatoes, tomato paste and fish, bring to boil. Reduce heat, simmer, uncovered, until fish is tender and sauce has thickened slightly.

Layer eggplants, fish mixture and cheese sauce in ovenproof dish (6 cup capacity), finishing with cheese sauce. Sprinkle with cheese, bake in moderate oven for about 30 minutes or until heated through and browned.

Cheese Sauce: Melt butter in medium saucepan, add flour, stir over medium heat for 1 minute (or microwave on HIGH for 1 minute). Remove from heat, gradually stir in milk, return to heat, stir constantly over high heat (or microwave on HIGH for about 3 minutes) or until mixture boils and thickens, stir in cheese.

Serves 6.

HEARTY FISH AND BEAN HOT POT

We used redfish fillets in this recipe. This dish is best prepared close to serving time. This recipe is not suitable to freeze or microwave.

¼ cup oil
3 medium potatoes, thickly sliced
750g white fish fillets, chopped
1 clove garlic, finely chopped
1 medium onion, coarsely chopped
½ teaspoon turmeric
3 tablespoons tomato paste
410g can tomatoes
1 small chicken stock cube, crumbled
1½ cups water
½ teaspoon dried oregano leaves
1 teaspoon sugar
310g can butter beans, drained
1 small lime, sliced
8 pitted black olives

Heat oil in large frying pan, gradually add potatoes to pan in single layer. Cook for about 3 minutes on each side or until golden brown and tender, drain on absorbent paper. Transfer potatoes to large saucepan.

Heat remaining oil in pan until very

Dish: Kitchen Collection

PAN-FRIED FISH WITH BACON MUSHROOM SAUCE

We used jewfish cutlets in this recipe. Fish must be cooked just before serving. Sauce can be made several hours before serving. This recipe is not suitable to freeze.

4 large white fish cutlets
plain flour
30g butter
BACON MUSHROOM SAUCE
3 bacon rashers, chopped
1 medium onion, chopped
⅔ cup thickened cream
2 green shallots, chopped
2 teaspoons cornflour
1 tablespoon water
75g baby mushrooms, sliced

Toss fish in flour, shake off excess flour. Heat butter in large frying pan, add fish in single layer, cook over medium heat for about 4 minutes on each side or until fish is tender. Serve with sauce.

Bacon Mushroom Sauce: Add bacon and onion to small saucepan, stir constantly over medium heat for about 2 minutes (or microwave on HIGH for about 3 minutes) or until onion is soft. Add cream, shallots and cornflour blended with water. Stir constantly over high heat (or microwave on HIGH for about 2 minutes) or until mixture boils and thickens. Add mushrooms, simmer for 1 minute (or microwave on HIGH for about 1 minute).

Serves 4.

hot, gradually add fish to pan in single layer. Cook over high heat until well-browned all over; drain on absorbent paper. Add fish to saucepan.

Reheat frying pan, add garlic, onion and turmeric, stir constantly over medium heat for about 2 minutes or until onion is soft. Stir in paste, undrained crushed tomatoes, stock cube, water, oregano and sugar. Bring to boil, reduce heat, simmer, uncovered, for about 3 minutes or until mixture is slightly thickened. Add beans, lime and olives, mix well.

Pour over fish and potatoes, mix gently. Bring to boil, reduce heat, simmer, covered, for about 5 minutes or until heated through.

Serves 4.

RIGHT: Pan-Fried Fish with Bacon Mushroom Sauce. ABOVE: From top: Hearty Fish and Bean Hot Pot; Layered Eggplant and Fish Casserole. LEFT: Crunchy-Topped Prawn and Asparagus Bake.

CHILLI SEAFOOD FRITTATA

We used ocean perch in this dish. Frittata is at its best made just before serving. This recipe is not suitable to freeze or microwave.

**375g white fish fillets
2 tablespoons oil
2 medium onions, sliced
1 large potato, grated
6 eggs, lightly beaten
1 tablespoon chopped fresh coriander
1 teaspoon chilli sauce**

Poach fish in large frying pan of simmering water, cook for about 3 minutes or until tender; drain and flake.

Heat oil in non-stick medium frying pan, add onions and potato, stir constantly over medium heat for about 3 minutes or until onions are soft. Add fish, stir until combined.

Stir in eggs, coriander and sauce, cook over low heat, without stirring, for about 2 minutes or until base is golden brown. Remove pan from heat, place under hot grill, cook until top of frittata is lightly browned.
Serves 4.

CREAMY SALMON WITH MUSHROOMS

This dish is best made just before serving. This recipe is not suitable to freeze or microwave.

**45g butter
375g baby mushrooms, chopped
130g can diced capsicum, drained
300ml carton cream
1 tablespoon seeded mustard
1 tablespoon chopped fresh chives
few drops tabasco sauce
2 green shallots, chopped
1 tablespoon brandy
2 teaspoons lemon juice
1½ tablespoons cornflour
½ cup water
440g can salmon, drained**

Heat butter in large saucepan, add mushrooms, cook, stirring occasionally, until mushrooms are tender. Add capsicum, cream, mustard, chives, sauce, shallots, brandy, juice and cornflour blended with water. Stir constantly over high heat until mixture boils and thickens. Add flaked salmon, stir gently until heated through. Serve with boiled rice.
Serves 4.

ANCHOVY, OLIVE AND ONION QUICHE

Prepare and cook quiche just before serving. This recipe is not suitable to freeze or microwave.

**30g butter
2 medium onions, sliced
8 sheets fillo pastry
60g butter, melted, extra
56g can anchovy fillets, drained, chopped
10 pitted black olives, chopped
3 eggs
300ml carton cream
½ cup milk
1 cup grated tasty cheese
1 tablespoon chopped fresh oregano**

Melt butter in small frying pan, add onions, cook over low heat for about 10 minutes or until onions are soft; stir occasionally; do not brown.

Brush each sheet of pastry with extra butter, layer pastry. Line deep 22cm flan tin with pastry, trim edge of pastry to fit tin. Spread onions, anchovies and olives into pastry case, stand tin on oven tray.

Whisk eggs in bowl with cream, milk, cheese and oregano, pour into pastry case. Bake in moderate oven for about 40 minutes or until filling is set and golden brown. Stand quiche for 5 minutes before serving.

WHOLEMEAL CREPES WITH CREAMY FISH FILLING

We used ling fillets in this recipe. Crêpes can be made up to a day ahead; keep, covered, in refrigerator. Crêpes can be frozen for up to 2 months layered with freezer or plastic wrap. Filling and sauce unsuitable to freeze or microwave.

CREPES
**¾ cup wholemeal plain flour
3 eggs, lightly beaten
1 tablespoon oil
1 cup milk**
CREAMY FISH FILLING
**500g white fish fillets, chopped
45g butter
1 small red pepper, chopped
2 tablespoons plain flour
1 cup milk
130g can corn kernels, drained
2 tablespoons chopped fresh chives**
TOMATO ONION SAUCE
**30g butter
1 medium onion, chopped
410g can tomatoes**

Crêpes: Sift flour into bowl, stir in combined eggs, oil and 2 tablespoons of the milk, beat until smooth; beat in remaining milk (or blend or process all ingredients until smooth). Cover, refrigerate for 30 minutes.

Heat small heavy-based frying pan, lightly grease. Pour 2 to 3 tablespoons of batter into pan, brown lightly underneath; turn, brown other side. Turn onto plate covered with greaseproof paper. Cover, keep warm in oven. Repeat with remaining batter. You will need about 12 crêpes for this recipe. Divide hot filling between crêpes. Serve with sauce.

Creamy Fish Filling: Poach fish in frying pan of simmering water for about 3 minutes or until tender, drain. Melt butter in medium saucepan, add pepper, stir over medium heat until soft. Stir in flour, stir constantly over medium heat for 1 minute. Remove from heat, gradually stir in milk, stir constantly over high heat until mixture boils and thickens. Add corn, chives and fish, stir until heated through.

Tomato Onion Sauce: Melt butter in small saucepan, add onion, stir constantly over medium heat for about 2 minutes or until onion is soft. Add undrained crushed tomatoes, bring to boil, reduce heat, simmer, uncovered, for about 5 minutes or until sauce is slightly thickened.

Serves 4.

ABOVE: From top: Creamy Salmon with Mushrooms; Chilli Seafood Frittata, Wholemeal Crêpes with Creamy Fish Filling. LEFT: Anchovy, Olive and Onion Quiche.

CRUSTY BAKED FISH CUTLETS

We used kingfish in this dish. Recipe can be prepared up to a day ahead; cook just before serving. This recipe is not suitable to freeze or microwave.

4 large white fish cutlets
2 tablespoons lemon juice
1 tablespoon dry white wine
⅔ cup stale breadcrumbs
1 cup grated tasty cheese
1 teaspoon dry mustard
4 green shallots, chopped
2 tablespoons chopped fresh parsley
1 tablespoon chopped fresh chives
1 tablespoon chopped fresh dill
1 clove garlic, crushed
60g butter, melted

Place fish in single layer in greased ovenproof dish, sprinkle with lemon juice and wine. Combine remaining ingredients in small bowl, spoon evenly over fish. Bake, uncovered, in moderate oven for about 40 minutes or until fish is tender.
   Serves 4.

BELOW: From Top: Crusty Baked Fish Cutlets; Pan-Fried Fish Cutlets with Creamy Corn Sauce. RIGHT: fish in Coconut Beer Batter.

PAN-FRIED FISH CUTLETS WITH CREAMY CORN SAUCE

We used blue-eyed cod cutlets in this recipe. Sauce can be made up to a day ahead; keep, covered in refrigerator. This recipe is not suitable to freeze.

4 large white fish cutlets
plain flour
30g butter
1 tablespoon oil
CREAMY CORN SAUCE
30g butter
1 medium onion, sliced
1 tablespoon plain flour
¾ cup water
1 small chicken stock cube, crumbled
130g can corn kernels, drained
¼ cup cream
2 tablespoons chopped fresh parsley

Toss cutlets in flour, shake off excess flour. Heat butter and oil in large frying pan, add fish to pan in single layer. Cook for about 5 minutes on each side until tender and browned; drain on absorbent paper. Serve with sauce.

Creamy Corn Sauce: Melt butter in small saucepan, add onion, stir constantly over medium heat for about 2 minutes (or microwave on HIGH for about 3 minutes) or until onion is soft. Add flour to pan, stir constantly over heat further minute (or microwave on HIGH for 1 minute). Remove from heat, gradually stir in combined water and stock cube, then corn, return to heat, stir constantly over high heat until sauce boils and thickens (or microwave on HIGH for about 2 minutes). Stir in cream and parsley, reheat before serving.
   Serves 4.

FISH IN COCONUT BEER BATTER

We used flathead in this recipe. Recipe unsuitable to freeze or microwave.

1 cup plain flour
1¼ cups beer
2 tablespoons coconut
1kg white fish fillets, chopped
plain flour, extra
oil for deep-frying
DIPPING SAUCE
⅓ cup sour cream
⅓ cup mayonnaise
¼ cup chopped stuffed olives
2 tablespoons tomato sauce

Sift flour into medium bowl, gradually stir in beer until smooth (or blend or process until smooth). Stir in coconut. Toss fish in extra flour, shake away excess flour. Dip fish into beer batter, deep-fry about 4 pieces at a time in hot oil until crisp and golden brown. Drain on absorbent paper. Serve with sauce and chips, if desired.

Dipping Sauce: Combine all ingredients in small bowl.
   Serves 4.

FISH MEUNIERE

We used bream fillets for this recipe. Cook fish as close to serving time as possible. This recipe is not suitable to freeze or microwave.

4 large white fish fillets
plain flour
155g butter
⅓ cup lemon juice
2 tablespoons chopped fresh parsley

Toss fish in flour, shake off excess flour. Heat half the butter in large frying pan, add fish, skin side up, in single layer. Cook for about 2 minutes on each side or until fish is tender. Remove from pan, keep warm. Melt remaining butter in pan, add juice and parsley, heat. Serve over fish.
Serves 4.

LEFT: Fish Meunière. BELOW: Tuna and Cashew Pilaf. RIGHT: From left: Creamy Salmon Sauce with Pasta; Seafood Curry Sauce with Pasta.

TUNA AND CASHEW PILAF

Pilaf is at its best made just before serving. This recipe is not suitable to freeze or microwave.

60g butter
1 medium onion, chopped
1½ cups long grain rice
2¼ cups water
2 small chicken stock cubes, crumbled
1 bay leaf
½ cup sultanas
1 cup cooked green peas
½ cup roasted unsalted cashews
440g can tuna in brine, drained

Melt butter in medium saucepan, add onion, stir constantly over medium heat for about 2 minutes or until onion is soft. Stir in rice, add water, stock cubes, bay leaf and sultanas. Bring to boil, reduce heat to very low, cover tightly, cook for about 20 minutes or until all liquid is absorbed and rice is tender. Using fork, gently stir rice; add peas, cashews and tuna, mix lightly. Remove bay leaf before serving.
Serves 4.

CREAMY SALMON SAUCE WITH PASTA

We used fettucine in this recipe. Make sauce close to serving time. This recipe is not suitable to freeze.

**440g can salmon, drained
15g butter
1 small onion, finely chopped
1 clove garlic, crushed
2 x 300ml cartons cream
1 small chicken stock cube, crumbled
1 teaspoon cornflour
1 tablespoon water
1 tablespoon lemon juice
1 tablespoon chopped fresh dill
375g pasta**

Flake salmon lightly with fork. Heat butter in medium saucepan, add onion and garlic, stir constantly over medium heat for about 1 minute (or microwave on HIGH for about 2 minutes) or until onion is soft. Add cream and stock cube, bring to boil. Blend cornflour with water, stir into pan, stir constantly over high heat (or microwave on HIGH for about 2 minutes) until mixture boils and thickens. Add salmon and juice.

Gradually add pasta to large saucepan of boiling water, boil, uncovered, for about 10 minutes or until just tender, drain. Stir hot salmon through pasta; sprinkle with dill.

Serves 6.

SEAFOOD CURRY SAUCE WITH PASTA

We used ocean perch fillets in this recipe. Curry sauce can be made up to a day ahead; keep, covered, in refrigerator. This recipe is not suitable to freeze or microwave.

**1 tablespoon oil
1 teaspoon yellow mustard seeds
¼ teaspoon cardamom seeds
1 clove garlic, finely chopped
1 medium onion, sliced
3 teaspoons curry powder
1 tablespoon sweet fruit chutney
1 tablespoon tomato paste
½ cup water
1 cup frozen peas
500g uncooked prawns, shelled
375g white fish fillets, chopped
250g cooked mussel meat, chopped
¼ cup coconut cream**

PARSLEY PASTA
**375g pasta
60g butter
1 teaspoon grated lemon rind
½ teaspoon paprika
1 tablespoon chopped fresh parsley**

Heat oil in large saucepan, add seeds, cover, cook over medium heat until seeds begin to crack. Add garlic and onion, stir constantly over medium heat for about 2 minutes or until onion is soft. Add curry powder, stir over heat for 1 minute. Add chutney, paste, water and peas, bring to boil, add prawns and fish. Reduce heat, simmer, covered, for about 5 minutes or until seafood is tender. Stir in mussels and cream, reheat without boiling. Serve with pasta.

Parsley Pasta: Add pasta gradually to large saucepan of boiling water, boil rapidly, uncovered, for about 10 minutes or until pasta is just tender; drain. Heat butter in large frying pan, add pasta, rind, paprika and parsley. Stir gently over heat until ingredients are combined.

Serves 6.

TASTY HERBED CRUMBED FISH

We used whiting fillets in this recipe. Fish can be crumbed up to several hours before cooking; keep, covered, in refrigerator. Mayonnaise can be prepared 2 days ahead. This recipe is not suitable to freeze or microwave.

**8 medium white fish fillets
plain flour
2 eggs, lightly beaten
2 tablespoons water
2 cups stale breadcrumbs
1 clove garlic, crushed
2 tablespoons chopped fresh parsley
1 tablespoon chopped fresh coriander
½ cup oil**

LEMON MUSTARD MAYONNAISE
**⅓ cup mayonnaise
1 teaspoon seeded mustard
2 tablespoons lemon juice**

Dust fish lightly with flour, shake off excess flour. Dip fish into combined eggs and water, then toss in combined breadcrumbs, garlic, parsley and coriander; press crumbs on firmly. Heat oil in large frying pan, add fish to pan in single layer. Fry over medium heat for about 5 minutes on each side or until fish is tender. Drain on absorbent paper, serve with lemon mustard mayonnaise.

Lemon Mustard Mayonnaise: Combine all ingredients in small bowl.
Serves 4.

HEARTY FISH CUTLETS WITH CHILLI BEAN SAUCE

Sauce can be prepared up to 2 hours ahead, cook fish just before serving. We used blue-eyed cod cutlets in this recipe. This recipe is not suitable to freeze or microwave.

**2 tablespoons oil
1 medium onion, chopped
1 clove garlic, crushed
425g can tomatoes
1 tablespoon tomato paste
½ cup dry red wine
1 teaspoon sugar
½ teaspoon chilli powder
315g can red kidney beans, rinsed, drained
1 medium green pepper, chopped
4 medium white fish cutlets
plain flour
30g butter
1 tablespoon oil, extra
1 tablespoon chopped fresh parsley**

Dishes: Balmain's Institute Arcade; tiles: Country Floors

Heat oil in large saucepan, add onion and garlic, stir constantly over heat for about 2 minutes or until onion is soft. Add undrained crushed tomatoes, tomato paste, wine, sugar and chilli powder. Bring to boil, reduce heat, simmer, uncovered, for about 20 minutes or until sauce is slightly thickened. Add beans and pepper, simmer for 5 minutes.

Lightly dust fish with flour, heat butter and extra oil in large frying pan, add fish to pan in single layer, cook on each side for about 5 minutes or until tender; drain on absorbent paper, serve with sauce. Sprinkle with parsley just before serving.

Serves 4.

ABOVE: Seafood in Rich Tomato Sauce.
LEFT: From top: Hearty Fish Cutlets with Chilli Bean Sauce; Tasty Herbed Crumbed Fish.

SEAFOOD IN RICH TOMATO SAUCE

This dish must be made just before serving. This recipe is not suitable to freeze or microwave.

**3 uncooked blue swimmer crabs
2 tablespoons oil
2 cloves garlic, crushed
1 medium onion, chopped
2 tablespoons tomato paste
½ cup dry red wine
2 x 425g can tomatoes
2 teaspoons sweet chilli sauce
1 teaspoon sugar
1 cup water
500g uncooked king prawns
250g scallops
250g squid rings
2 tablespoons chopped fresh parsley
1 tablespoon cornflour
¼ cup water, extra**

Crack nippers of crabs slightly, chop down centre of crabs to cut in half.

Heat oil in large deep saucepan, add garlic and onion, stir constantly over medium heat for about 2 minutes or until onion is soft. Stir in tomato paste, wine, undrained crushed tomatoes, chilli sauce, sugar and water. Bring to boil, reduce heat; simmer, uncovered, for 10 minutes.

Add crab to tomato mixture, bring to boil, reduce heat; simmer, covered, for 5 minutes.

Shell and devein prawns, leaving tails intact. Stir prawns, scallops and squid into tomato mixture. Bring to boil, reduce heat, simmer few minutes or until seafood is cooked; add parsley. Blend cornflour with extra water, stir into tomato mixture, stir constantly over high heat until mixture boils and thickens.

Serves 4.

FISH AND MACARONI PIE

We used ling fish fillets in this recipe. Pie can be prepared up to a day ahead; keep, covered, in refrigerator. This recipe is not suitable to freeze.

**250g macaroni
30g butter
1 cup grated tasty cheese
1 egg, lightly beaten**
TOMATO FISH SAUCE
**500g white fish fillets
30g butter
4 green shallots, chopped
1 clove garlic, crushed
425g can tomatoes
½ cup dry white wine
½ cup water
1 large vegetable stock cube, crumbled
2 tablespoons chopped fresh parsley**
WHITE SAUCE
**45g butter
⅓ cup plain flour
1½ cups milk**

Add macaroni to large saucepan of boiling water, boil, uncovered, until just tender; drain. Melt butter in pan, add macaroni, mix well, cool 5 minutes. Stir in half the cheese and egg.

Pour half the macaroni mixture into greased 23cm square ovenproof dish, top with tomato fish sauce, then remaining macaroni mixture. Pour white sauce over macaroni, sprinkle with remaining cheese. Bake in moderate oven for about 45 minutes or until golden brown. Stand 10 minutes before serving.

Tomato Fish Sauce: Add fish to medium frying pan of simmering water, cook for 3 minutes; drain and flake. Melt butter in pan, add shallots and garlic, cook for 2 minutes over medium heat or until shallots are soft. Add undrained crushed tomatoes, wine, water and stock cube, bring to boil, reduce heat, simmer, uncovered, for about 20 minutes or until slightly reduced. Stir in fish and parsley.

White Sauce: Melt butter in small saucepan, add flour, stir over heat for 1 minute (or microwave on HIGH for 1 minute), remove from heat. Gradually stir in milk constantly over high heat (or microwave on HIGH for about 2 minutes) or until white sauce boils and thickens.

Serves 6.

SALMON AND VEGETABLE SAUCE WITH PASTA

We used tagliatelle in this recipe. Sauce is best made just before serving. Recipe unsuitable to freeze.

**500g broccoli, chopped
30g butter
1 medium onion, sliced
1 medium red pepper, chopped
2 small zucchini, sliced
1½ tablespoons plain flour
300ml carton cream
½ cup water
½ teaspoon grated lemon rind
1 tablespoon lemon juice
¼ cup dry white wine
130g can corn kernels, drained
425g can salmon, drained, flaked
375g pasta**

Boil, steam or microwave broccoli until just tender, drain. Heat butter in large frying pan, add onion, pepper and zucchini, stir constantly over medium heat for about 2 minutes (or microwave on HIGH for 3 minutes) or until onion and zucchini are soft.

Add flour to pan, stir over medium heat for 1 minute, remove from heat. Gradually stir in combined cream, water, lemon rind and juice and wine, return to heat. Stir constantly over high heat (or microwave on HIGH for about 3 minutes) until mixture boils and thickens. Add broccoli, corn and salmon, stir until heated through.

Add pasta gradually to large saucepan of boiling water, boil, uncovered, for about 10 minutes or until tender, drain. Serve hot sauce over hot pasta.

Serves 6.

WHOLE FISH WITH VEGETABLE SEASONING

We used snapper in this recipe. Fish can be seasoned a day ahead; keep, covered, in refrigerator. This recipe is not suitable to freeze.

**4 small whole white fish
60g butter
1 stick celery, finely chopped
1 small carrot, finely chopped
1 small onion, finely chopped
1 clove garlic, crushed
1 cup stale breadcrumbs
2 tablespoons lemon juice
1 tablespoon oil
¼ cup water**
PARSLEY AND CHEESE SAUCE
**15g butter
1 tablespoon plain flour
1 cup milk
½ cup grated tasty cheese
2 tablespoons chopped fresh parsley**

Make 2 or 3 slashes across each side of fish in the thickest part. Melt butter in medium saucepan, add celery, carrot, onion and garlic. Stir constantly over medium heat for about 5 minutes (or microwave on HIGH for about 5 minutes) or until vegetables are soft; stir in breadcrumbs.

Fill cavity of each fish with seasoning. Place fish in single layer in large baking dish. Pour combined juice, oil and water over fish. Bake, uncovered, in moderate oven for about 20 minutes (or microwave on HIGH for about 15 minutes) or until fish are tender; baste fish several times during cooking. Serve with sauce.

Parsley and Cheese Sauce: Melt butter in small saucepan, stir in flour, stir constantly over medium heat for 1 minute (or microwave on HIGH for 1 minute). Remove from heat, gradually stir in milk, stir constantly over high heat (or microwave on HIGH for about 2 minutes) or until sauce boils and thickens. Remove from heat, stir in cheese and parsley.

Serves 4.

RIGHT: Whole Fish with Vegetable Seasoning. ABOVE: From left: Salmon and Vegetable Sauce with Pasta; Fish and Macaroni Pie.

FISH AND POTATO SCALLOPS WITH TARTARE SAUCE

We used bream in this recipe. This recipe is not suitable to freeze or microwave.

3 medium potatoes
2 cups self-raising flour
1 egg, lightly beaten
1½ cups water
4 medium white fish fillets
cornflour
oil for deep-frying
TARTARE SAUCE
¾ cup mayonnaise
¼ cup cream
2 tablespoons chopped gherkins
2 tablespoons drained capers, chopped
2 tablespoons chopped fresh chives

Boil, steam or microwave potatoes until just tender; cool, cut into 1cm-thick slices. Sift flour into medium bowl, make well in centre, gradually stir in egg and water (or blend or process ingredients) until smooth.

Dip fish and potatoes into cornflour, shake away excess cornflour. Dip into batter, deep-fry in hot oil until golden brown and tender. Drain on absorbent paper. Serve with sauce and chips.

Tartare Sauce: Combine all ingredients in small bowl.

Serves 4.

SMOKED FISH AND VEGETABLE PIE

We used smoked haddock in this dish. Pie filling can be prepared a day ahead; keep, covered, in refrigerator. Place pastry in position just before cooking. This recipe is not suitable to freeze.

2 cups milk
1 small onion, finely chopped
30g butter
¼ cup plain flour
750g smoked fish, chopped
250g frozen mixed thawed vegetables
¼ cup chopped fresh parsley
1 egg, lightly beaten
1 sheet ready-rolled puff pastry

Combine milk and onion in medium saucepan, bring to boil. Reduce heat,

PAN-FRIED FISH WITH SWEET AND SOUR SAUCE

We used ocean perch fillets in this recipe. Sauce can be prepared several hours ahead; keep, covered, in refrigerator. Cook fish just before serving. This recipe is not suitable to freeze or microwave.

**225g can sweetened pineapple pieces
1 tablespoon oil
1 clove garlic, crushed
1 teaspoon grated fresh ginger
1 medium onion, coarsely chopped
1 small red pepper, chopped
1 small green pepper, chopped
1 stick celery, chopped
2 teaspoons cornflour
⅓ cup tomato sauce
2 teaspoons light soy sauce
1 teaspoon sweet chilli sauce
1 tablespoon white vinegar
4 medium white fish fillets
plain flour
30g butter**

Drain pineapple, reserve ¼ cup syrup. Heat oil in medium frying pan, add garlic, ginger and onion, stir-fry over medium heat for about 2 minutes or until onion is just soft. Add peppers, celery and pineapple pieces, stir-fry for 1 minute. Stir in cornflour blended with reserved syrup, sauces and vinegar, stir constantly over high heat until sauce boils and thickens.

Toss fish in flour, shake off excess flour. Heat butter in large pan, add fish in single layer, cook on both sides for about 3 minutes or until fish is tender. Serve fish fillets with hot sauce.

Serves 4.

BELOW: From top: Smoked Fish and Vegetable Pie; Pan-Fried Fish with Sweet and Sour Sauce. LEFT: Fish and Potato Scallops with Tartare Sauce.

simmer 5 minutes. Melt butter in large saucepan, add flour, stir constantly over medium heat for 1 minute (or microwave on HIGH for 1 minute), remove from heat. Gradually stir in milk mixture, return to heat, stir constantly over high heat, (or microwave on HIGH for about 3 minutes) or until mixture boils and thickens.

Add fish, vegetables and parsley, pour into ovenproof dish (4 cup capacity). Brush edges of dish with egg, cover dish with pastry. Press pastry firmly around edge of dish, trim, decorate with scraps of pastry, if desired. Brush with egg. Bake in moderately hot oven for about 25 minutes or until pastry is brown.

Serves 4.

SNACKS AND LUNCHES

Here are little, light, tasty seafood meals for families on the go, for casual entertaining and for weekends when the kids bring their friends home after sport. Whatever the occasion, you will find delicious ideas in our big cross-section of recipes.

SWEET BUG TAIL STIR-FRY

Stir-fry is best made just before serving. Recipe unsuitable to freeze.

**8 uncooked Balmain bugs
1 tablespoon oil
1 medium onion, quartered
1 clove garlic, crushed
200g broccoli, chopped
1 stick celery, chopped
1 medium carrot, thinly sliced
1 medium red pepper, sliced
450g can sweetened pineapple pieces, drained
2 teaspoons cornflour
1 tablespoon water
1 tablespoon hoisin sauce
1 tablespoon light soy sauce
1 tablespoon barbecue sauce
½ teaspoon tabasco sauce
2 tablespoons honey**

Remove flesh from Balmain bug tails, cut into half lengthways. Heat oil in wok or frying pan (or microwave on HIGH for 1 minute), add onion and garlic. Stir-fry constantly over high heat for about 2 minutes (or microwave on HIGH for 3 minutes) or until onion is just soft. Add remaining vegetables, pineapple and Balmain bug tails, stir-fry over high heat for 2 minutes (or microwave on HIGH for 2 minutes).

Blend cornflour with water in jug, add sauces and honey, add to pan, stir constantly over high heat (or microwave on HIGH for about 2 minutes) until mixture boils and thickens slightly.

Serves 4.

FISH AND CARROT ROLLS WITH MINT CORIANDER SAUCE

We used redfish fillets in this recipe. Fish and chicken can be marinated up to a day ahead; keep, covered, in refrigerator or freeze for a month. This recipe is unsuitable to freeze or microwave.

**375g white fish fillets
250g chicken breast fillets, chopped
2 tablespoons sweet sherry
2 green shallots, finely chopped
1 teaspoon chopped fresh dill
2 medium carrots, finely grated
3 eggs
1½ tablespoons water**
MINT CORIANDER SAUCE
**1 cup water
1 small chicken stock cube, crumbled
1 tablespoon chopped fresh mint
1 teaspoon chopped fresh coriander
1 clove garlic, crushed
2 teaspoons honey
2 teaspoons cornflour
1 tablespoon water, extra
1 tablespoon chopped fresh chives**

Combine fish, chicken and sherry in medium bowl, cover, refrigerate for about 2 hours or overnight.

Blend or process undrained fish mixture until smooth, transfer to medium bowl, mix in shallots and dill. Squeeze excess liquid from carrots; discard liquid. Beat eggs and water with fork until combined.

Heat wok or large frying pan, lightly oil wok or pan, pour in a quarter of the egg mixture to make an omelette about 15cm diameter. Tilt wok or pan from side to side to make omelette as round as possible, cook until omelette is just set. Remove from wok. Make 3 more omelettes with the remaining egg mixture.

Place omelettes on flat surface, divide fish mixture evenly between omelettes. Spread each omelette with fish mixture to about 2cm from edge. Top fish mixture with carrot; roll up omelette firmly.

Place wire rack in baking or flameproof dish, add enough boiling water to come within 2cm of the rack. Place rolls in single layer, seam side down, on rack. Cover, steam for about 10 minutes or until rolls are tender. Slice diagonally into thick pieces, serve with mint coriander sauce.

Mint Coriander Sauce: Combine water, stock cube, mint, coriander, garlic and honey in small saucepan. Bring to boil, reduce heat, simmer, uncovered, for about 10 minutes or until about a quarter of the liquid is evaporated. Strain, return liquid to clean saucepan, stir in cornflour blended with extra water. Stir constantly over high heat until sauce boils and thickens; stir in chives.

Serves 4.

From top: Sweet Bug Tail Stir-Fry; Fish and Carrot Rolls with Mint Coriander Sauce.

CRUSTY BAKED SMOKED SALMON PUFF

Serve puff as soon as it is cooked; it will deflate on standing. Recipe unsuitable to freeze or microwave.

1 loaf unsliced white bread
60g butter, melted
¾ cup milk
30g butter, extra
125g smoked salmon, chopped
3 green shallots, chopped
1 tablespoon drained capers
1 tablespoon chopped fresh parsley
1½ cups (185g) grated tasty cheese
4 eggs

Lightly grease base of deep 22cm flan tin. Remove crusts from bread, cut bread into 3 × 1½cm slices. Trim bread to fit around side of tin. Brush both sides of bread with melted butter; line tin with bread. Place tin on oven tray. Blend or process remaining bread until finely crumbed.

Bring milk to boil in large saucepan, remove from heat, stir in extra butter, salmon, shallots, capers, parsley, cheese and 1½ cups of the breadcrumbs; transfer to large bowl.

Beat eggs in small bowl with electric mixer for about 10 minutes or until eggs are thick and creamy. Gently fold into salmon mixture, pour into prepared tin. Bake in moderate oven for about 1 hour or until puffed and golden brown.

TASTY PRAWN TOASTED SANDWICHES

Filling can be prepared up to 2 hours ahead; keep, covered, in refrigerator. This recipe is not suitable to freeze or microwave.

8 slices bread
butter
250g cooked shelled prawns, finely chopped
¼ cup mayonnaise
1 cup grated tasty cheese
2 green shallots, chopped
½ teaspoon dry mustard
1 tablespoon tomato paste
2 teaspoons chopped fresh dill
few drops tabasco sauce

Spread bread evenly with butter on 1 side. Combine remaining ingredients in medium bowl, spoon over unbuttered side of half the slices. Top with remaining slices, buttered side up. Place sandwiches in jaffle iron or sandwich maker, cook until golden brown on both sides.
Makes 4.

FISH AND SPAGHETTI FRITTATA

We used gemfish in this recipe. Make frittata just before serving. Recipe unsuitable to freeze or microwave.

200g spaghetti
30g butter
½ cup grated tasty cheese
½ cup grated parmesan cheese
4 green shallots, chopped
1 teaspoon curry powder
½ teaspoon dried mixed herbs
2 tablespoons chopped fresh parsley
6 eggs, lightly beaten
350g white fish fillets, finely chopped
¼ cup milk
60g butter, extra

Cook spaghetti in large saucepan of boiling water for about 12 minutes or until tender; drain. Place hot spaghetti into large bowl, stir in butter, cheeses, shallots, curry powder, herbs, parsley, eggs, fish and milk.

Heat half the extra butter in large frying pan, add spaghetti mixture, spread evenly into pan. Cook over medium heat until well-browned; invert onto large greased plate. Add remaining butter to pan then return frittata to pan with browned side up. Cook other side until well browned. Slide onto plate before cutting.
Serves 4 to 6.

ABOVE: Left: Tasty Prawn Toasted Sandwiches; right: Fish and Spaghetti Frittata. BELOW LEFT: Crusty Baked Smoked Salmon Puff.

SALMON AND CREAM CHEESE ROLLUPS

Salmon mixture can be prepared up to a day ahead; keep, covered, in refrigerator. Rolls can be prepared up to several hours before serving. This recipe is not suitable to freeze.

250g packet cream cheese
¼ cup mayonnaise
2 tablespoons lemon juice
210g can salmon, drained
2 rounds flat bread
3 medium gherkins, chopped
2 cups alfalfa sprouts

Blend or process cheese, mayonnaise and lemon juice until smooth. Add salmon, blend until smooth. Split each piece of bread into 2 rounds. Spread each round with salmon mixture, sprinkle with gherkins and sprouts, roll up bread. Refrigerate before serving.
Makes 4.

COLD SALMON AND EGG PIE

Pie can be made up to 4 days ahead; it is at its best a day after making; keep, covered, in refrigerator. This recipe is not suitable to freeze or microwave.

1 tablespoon drained capers
2 × 440g cans salmon, drained
4 hard-boiled eggs
1 egg yolk, extra
1 tablespoon milk
HOT WATER PASTRY
3 cups plain flour
2 egg yolks
125g lard
⅔ cup water
PARSLEY JELLY
1½ tablespoons gelatine
1 cup water
½ cup dry white wine
2 teaspoons chopped fresh parsley

Grease base and side of deep 17cm round cake pan.

Roll out two-thirds of the pastry large enough to line base and side of prepared cake pan. Press pastry firmly into pan, making sure there are no cracks or holes.

Combine capers and flaked salmon in medium bowl, place into pastry case with eggs.

Roll out remaining pastry to cover top of pan, brush edges with combined egg yolk and milk. Press edges together firmly with fork. Cut a small hole, about 2cm wide, in top of pastry, brush top with egg mixture. Bake in hot oven for 30 minutes or until golden brown, reduce heat to moderate, bake further 15 minutes. If necessary, cover top of pie with foil to prevent pastry becoming too dark.

Stand pie for 10 minutes, then pour parsley jelly into the pie, topping up occasionally with jelly until the pie is as full as possible; cool to room temperature. Refrigerate overnight.

Hot Water Pastry: Sift flour into large bowl, make well in centre, add egg yolks, cover with some of the flour.

Place lard and water into small saucepan, stir over low heat until lard is melted, bring to boil. Pour boiling liquid into flour all at once; mix to a firm dough with wooden spoon.

Turn onto lightly floured surface, knead lightly until smooth. Cover pastry with cloth, stand for 10 minutes. Knead again until smooth.

Parsley Jelly: Sprinkle gelatine over water in small bowl, stand in small pan of simmering water, stir until dissolved (or microwave on HIGH for 30 seconds). Stir in wine and parsley.

SALMON BAGELS

Cream cheese mixture can be prepared up to a day ahead; allow to return to room temperature before using. This recipe is not suitable to freeze or microwave.

125g packet cream cheese
1 teaspoon grated lemon rind
1 tablespoon lemon juice
1 tablespoon chopped fresh dill
4 bagels
shredded lettuce
210g can salmon, drained
1 small red Spanish onion, sliced
1 tablespoon drained capers

Beat cream cheese in small bowl with electric mixer until light and creamy. Add lemon rind, juice and dill, beat until combined. Split bagels, spread cut sides with cream cheese mixture, top 4 halves with lettuce, flaked salmon, onion and capers, top with remaining bagel halves.
Makes 4.

SMOKED FISH AND SAFFRON RICE SLICE

We used smoked cod in this recipe. Slice can be prepared several hours ahead. Recipe unsuitable to freeze.

3 cups water
1 small chicken stock cube, crumbled
tiny pinch saffron powder
⅔ cup long grain rice
1 egg, lightly beaten
375g smoked fish
2 eggs, lightly beaten, extra
¾ cup milk
¾ cup grated tasty cheese
1 medium zucchini, grated
1 teaspoon French mustard
1 tablespoon chopped fresh chives

Bring water to boil in large saucepan, add stock cube, saffron and rice, reduce heat, simmer, covered, over low heat for about 20 minutes or until all liquid has been absorbed and rice is tender; cool 5 minutes. Stir in egg.

Spread rice mixture evenly over base of greased foil-lined 19cm x 29cm lamington pan or ovenproof dish.

Cook fish in frying pan of simmering water for about 3 minutes. Drain and flake with fork, spread over rice. Pour over combined extra eggs, milk, cheese, zucchini, mustard and chives. Bake in moderate oven for about 40 minutes or until golden brown and set (or microwave on MEDIUM for about 15 minutes or until set). Stand for 5 minutes before serving.

ABOVE: Cold Salmon and Egg Pie. RIGHT: Clockwise from top: Salmon Bagels; Salmon and Cream Cheese Rollups; Smoked Fish and Saffron Rice Slice.

Plates: Casa Shopping; spoon and lace napkins: Cottage Antiques

SMOKED FISH AND VEGETABLE CAKE

We used smoked haddock in this recipe. This dish is best made just before serving, although the cooked cake can be frozen for up to 2 months.

**60g butter
1 medium onion, finely chopped
2 teaspoons curry powder
200g broccoli, chopped
125g baby mushrooms, thinly sliced
500g smoked fish, chopped
1 cup white self-raising flour
½ cup wholemeal self-raising flour
2 eggs, lightly beaten
¾ cup milk
1 cup grated tasty cheese
2 tablespoons cracked wheat
CHEESY MUSTARD SAUCE
30g butter
2 tablespoons plain flour
1½ cups milk
¼ cup grated tasty cheese
1 teaspoon seeded mustard**

Grease deep 20cm round cake pan, cover base with greaseproof paper, grease paper. Heat butter in frying pan, add onion and curry powder. Stir constantly over medium heat for about 2 minutes (or microwave on HIGH for about 3 minutes) or until onion is soft. Add broccoli, mushrooms and fish, stir constantly over heat further 2 minutes (or microwave on HIGH for about 3 minutes).

Sift flours into bowl, make well in centre, add vegetable mixture, eggs and milk and half the cheese. Stir until mixture is just combined.

Spread mixture into prepared pan, sprinkle with remaining cheese and cracked wheat. Bake in moderate oven for about 1¼ hours or until firm to touch. Stand 5 minutes before turning out, serve with sauce.

Cheesy Mustard Sauce: Melt butter in saucepan (or microwave on HIGH for 1 minute), stir in flour, stir constantly over medium heat for 1 minute (or microwave on HIGH for 1 minute). Remove from heat, gradually add milk, stir constantly over high heat (or microwave on HIGH for about 3 minutes) until mixture boils and thickens. Remove from heat, stir in cheese and mustard.

Plates: Pottery Plus

TUNA AND CORN PLAIT

Make plait just before cooking; it can be frozen for up to 2 months. Sauce can be made up to 2 days ahead; or frozen for up to 2 months. Recipe unsuitable to microwave.

**2 cups self-raising flour
30g butter
1 egg, lightly beaten
½ cup milk, approximately
1 tablespoon grated tasty cheese
TUNA AND CORN FILLING
425g can tuna in brine, drained
130g can corn kernels, drained
½ cup grated tasty cheese
VEGETABLE SAUCE
15g butter
1 tablespoon plain flour
1½ cups milk
1 sachet Vegetable
    Cup.a.Soup Mix**

Lightly grease 14cm x 21cm loaf pan, line base with greaseproof paper, grease paper.

Sift flour into large bowl, rub in butter, stir in egg and enough milk to mix to a firm, pliable dough. Turn onto lightly floured surface, knead lightly until smooth.

Divide dough into 3 portions, roll each portion into a roll about 30cm long; flatten each roll slightly. Place one-third of the filling along centre of each roll, fold edges over to enclose filling, then reshape each roll. Plait rolls firmly, pinching ends together.

Place into prepared pan, brush top with a little milk, sprinkle with cheese. Bake in hot oven 25 minutes, reduce to moderate, bake further 20 minutes or until golden brown. Stand 5 minutes before turning out. Serve with sauce.

Tuna and Corn Filling: Combine all ingredients in medium bowl.

Vegetable Sauce: Melt butter in small saucepan, add flour, stir constantly over medium heat for 30 seconds. Remove from heat, gradually stir in combined milk and soup mix. Return to heat, stir constantly over high heat until mixture boils and thickens.

QUICK FISH CROUSTADE

We used gemfish fillets in this recipe. Sauce can be prepared up to a day ahead; keep, covered, in refrigerator. This recipe is not suitable to freeze.

4 bread rolls
30g butter, melted
2 tablespoons oil
1 medium onion, chopped
1 clove garlic, crushed
1 medium green pepper, chopped
410g can tomatoes
2 tablespoons chopped fresh parsley
1 teaspoon chopped fresh thyme
375g white fish fillets, chopped

Cut tops from rolls, hollow out centre of rolls. Brush inside of rolls and lids with butter, place on ungreased oven tray, bake in moderate oven for about 5 minutes or until crisp.

Heat oil in medium saucepan, add onion and garlic, stir constantly over heat for about 2 minutes (or microwave on HIGH for about 3 minutes) or until onion is soft. Stir in pepper, undrained crushed tomatoes, parsley, thyme and fish. Bring to boil, reduce heat, simmer for about 5 minutes (or microwave on HIGH for about 3 minutes) or until mixture is slightly thickened.

Fill rolls with mixture, top with lids, return to tray. Bake, uncovered, in moderate oven for about 15 minutes or until heated through.

Makes 4.

TUNA, TOMATO AND PASTA MINI CASSEROLES

Any type of pasta or macaroni can be used in this recipe. Casseroles can be prepared ready for baking a day ahead; keep, covered, in refrigerator. Recipe unsuitable to freeze or microwave.

375g pasta
1 tablespoon oil
1 medium onion, chopped
2 cloves garlic, crushed
2 tablespoons tomato paste
410g can tomatoes
415g can tomato purée
425g can tuna in brine, drained
2 tablespoons chopped fresh chives
1½ cups (185g) grated tasty cheese
1 cup grated mozzarella cheese

Add pasta gradually to large saucepan of boiling water, boil rapidly, uncovered, until tender; drain.

Heat oil in large saucepan, add onion and garlic, stir constantly over medium heat for about 2 minutes or until onion is soft. Add tomato paste, undrained crushed tomatoes and purée. Bring to boil, reduce heat, simmer, uncovered, for about 15 minutes or until mixture is slightly thickened. Stir in tuna, chives, tasty cheese and pasta.

Spoon mixture into 6 ovenproof dishes (1 cup capacity). Sprinkle with mozzarella cheese, bake in moderate oven for about 15 minutes or until lightly browned.

Serves 6.

BELOW: From left: Quick Fish Croustade; Tuna, Tomato and Pasta Mini Casseroles. FAR LEFT: From top: Tuna and Corn Plait; Smoked Fish and Vegetable Cake.

CRUSTY-TOPPED SALMON BAKE

Salmon bake can be prepared several hours ahead of cooking time. This recipe is not suitable to freeze or microwave.

15g butter
1 small onion, finely chopped
1 small red pepper, finely chopped
1 clove garlic, crushed
1 large carrot, grated
440g can salmon, drained
5 slices stale white bread
4 eggs
300ml carton cream
2 tablespoons chopped fresh parsley
1 cup grated tasty cheese

Heat butter in frying pan, add onion, pepper, garlic and carrot. Stir constantly over medium heat for about 5 minutes or until carrot is soft; stir in salmon. Place into greased ovenproof dish (4 cup capacity).

Remove crusts from bread, cut into triangles, cover salmon mixture with bread. Beat eggs, cream and parsley together in bowl, pour over bread, sprinkle with cheese. Bake in moderate oven for about 30 minutes or until golden brown.

Serves 4.

OPEN SANDWICHES

We used rye bread for these sandwiches. Assemble sandwiches as close as possible to serving time. This recipe is not suitable to freeze.

PRAWN AND STRAWBERRY SALAD
8 slices bread
60g butter, softened
1 small lettuce
400g cooked prawns, shelled
½ × 250g punnet strawberries, sliced
½ × 250g punnet cherry tomatoes, quartered
DRESSING
¼ cup mayonnaise
1 tablespoon tomato sauce
1 teaspoon drained capers, chopped
1 teaspoon horseradish cream
SARDINE AND RADISH SALAD
8 slices bread
60g butter, softened
1 small lettuce
2 × 120g cans sardines, drained
4 radishes, chopped
1 small carrot, grated
250g punnet cherry tomatoes, quartered
DRESSING
2 tablespoons mayonnaise
1 tablespoon sour cream
1 teaspoon seeded mustard
2 teaspoons lemon juice

Prawn and Strawberry Salad: Spread bread evenly with butter, top with lettuce, prawns, strawberries and tomatoes, then dressing.
Dressing: Combine all ingredients in small bowl.
Sardine and Radish Salad: Spread bread evenly with butter, top with lettuce, sardines, radishes, carrot and tomatoes, then dressing.
Dressing: Combine all ingredients in small bowl.

Makes 16.

OCEAN TROUT AND CRAB TERRINE

Atlantic salmon can be used instead of ocean trout, if preferred.
Make terrine up to 2 days ahead; keep, covered, in refrigerator. Recipe unsuitable to freeze or microwave.

CRAB MOUSSE
400g uncooked prawns, shelled
2 × 200g cans crab, drained
1 egg white
½ cup cream
2 tablespoons chopped fresh dill
TROUT MOUSSE
400g ocean trout
1 egg white
300ml carton thickened cream
CREAMY DILL MAYONNAISE
1 egg yolk
2 teaspoons white vinegar
½ cup oil
3 teaspoons tomato sauce
2 teaspoons chopped fresh dill

Crab Mousse: Line base and sides of ovenproof (not metal) loaf dish (base measures 10cm × 20cm) with plastic wrap. Process prawns, crab and egg white until smooth. Add cream and dill, process until just combined. Refrigerate the mixture while preparing trout mousse.

Spread half the crab mousse evenly into prepared dish, top with half the trout mousse. Repeat layering with remaining crab and trout mousses. Cover with plastic wrap, then foil.

Place terrine in baking dish with enough boiling water to come halfway up sides of dish. Bake in moderate oven for about 1½ hours or until firm to touch. Cool to room temperature; refrigerate overnight.

Trout Mousse: Process trout and egg white until smooth. Add cream, process only until just combined.

Creamy Dill Mayonnaise: Combine egg yolk and vinegar in medium bowl, gradually whisk in oil in thin steady stream; whisk constantly until combined. Stir in sauce and dill.

ABOVE: From top: Crusty-Topped Salmon Bake; Open Sandwiches. RIGHT: Ocean Trout and Crab Terrine.

Spoon: Cottage Antiques

China: Limoges; tiles: Country Floors

79

CRUNCHY-COATED FISH LOAF

Fish loaf is at its best made as close as possible to serving time, although it can be made several hours ahead. This recipe is not suitable to freeze.

15g butter
½ cup packaged breadcrumbs
2 tablespoons grated parmesan cheese
500g white fish fillets, chopped
1 medium onion, coarsely chopped
1 medium carrot, coarsely grated
1 tablespoon chopped fresh chives
1 teaspoon grated lemon rind
1 tablespoon lemon juice
½ cup mayonnaise
2 cups stale breadcrumbs
2 eggs

Grease 14cm x 21cm loaf pan or ovenproof dish. Melt butter in frying pan, add packaged breadcrumbs, stir constantly over medium heat until lightly browned. Stand for 5 minutes. Stir in cheese. Sprinkle base and sides of pan with half the cheese and breadcrumb mixture, reserve remaining cheese and breadcrumb mixture.

Blend or process remaining ingredients until smooth, spread into prepared pan, press remaining cheese and breadcrumb mixture onto loaf. Bake in moderate oven for about 45 minutes or until loaf is firm (or microwave on MEDIUM for about 20 minutes). Stand loaf for 15 minutes before turning out.

CUCUMBER AND SALMON MOULD

Dish can be made up to 2 days ahead; keep, covered, in refrigerator. Recipe unsuitable to freeze or microwave.

1 large cucumber, peeled
440g can salmon, drained
3 green shallots, chopped
1 teaspoon grated lime rind
2 teaspoons lime juice
⅓ cup thickened cream
1 tablespoon seeded mustard
130g can creamed corn
1½ tablespoons gelatine
⅓ cup water
CUCUMBER SOUR CREAM SAUCE
1 small cucumber, peeled
½ cup sour cream
1 tablespoon chopped fresh chives
1 tablespoon chopped fresh mint

Halve cucumber, remove seeds with teaspoon; roughly chop cucumber. Blend or process salmon, cucumber, shallots, rind and juice until smooth. Transfer mixture to a medium bowl, stir in cream, mustard and corn.

Sprinkle gelatine over water in small bowl, stand in small pan of simmering water, stir until dissolved; cool.

Stir gelatine mixture into salmon mixture; spread evenly into mould (4 cup capacity), cover, refrigerate for several hours or overnight. Turn onto serving plate, serve with sauce.

Cucumber Sour Cream Sauce: Remove seeds from cucumber, finely chop cucumber, combine in medium bowl with cream and herbs.

Serves 4.

HERBED FISH ROLL WITH CHUNKY TOMATO SAUCE

We used gemfish fillets in this recipe. Roll is best made as close as possible to serving time. Sauce can be made up to a day ahead; keep, covered, in refrigerator. This recipe is not suitable to freeze or microwave.

2 cups self-raising flour
30g butter
¾ cup milk, approximately
1 egg, lightly beaten
1 tablespoon grated parmesan cheese
FILLING
250g white fish fillets, chopped
1 egg
3 green shallots, chopped
1 tablespoon chopped fresh parsley
2 teaspoons chopped fresh dill
½ teaspoon grated lemon rind
2 teaspoons lemon juice
1 small green pepper, chopped
CHUNKY TOMATO SAUCE
1 tablespoon oil
1 medium onion, thinly sliced
1 clove garlic, crushed
1 medium red pepper, chopped
410g can tomatoes
1 tablespoon brown sugar
2 teaspoons cornflour
⅓ cup water

Sift flour into large bowl, rub in butter. Add enough milk to mix to a soft dough. Turn dough onto lightly floured surface, knead lightly until smooth. roll to 20cm x 30cm rectangle. Spread evenly with filling, leaving about 2cm around edges, brush edges with egg.

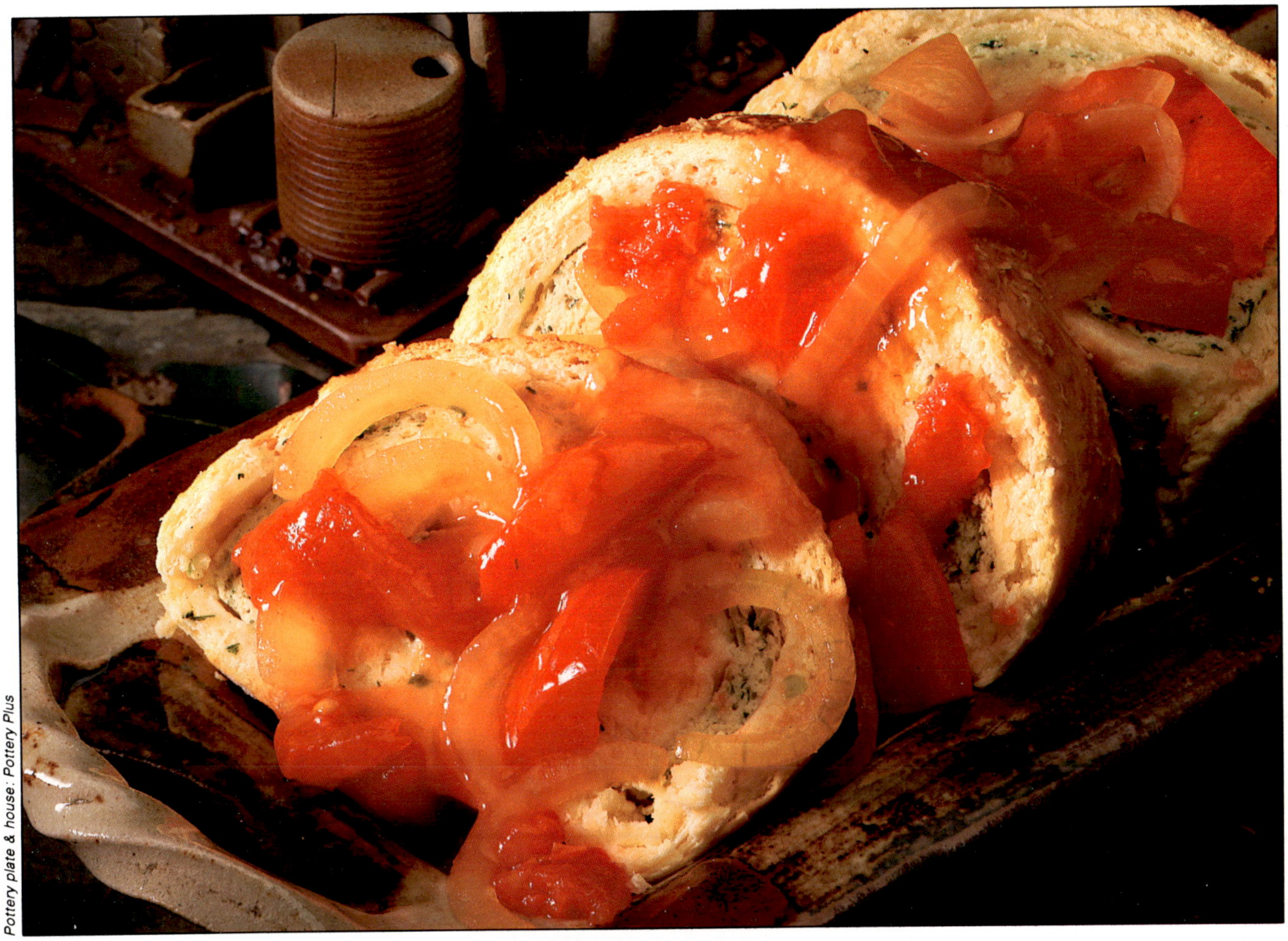

Pottery plate & house: Pottery Plus

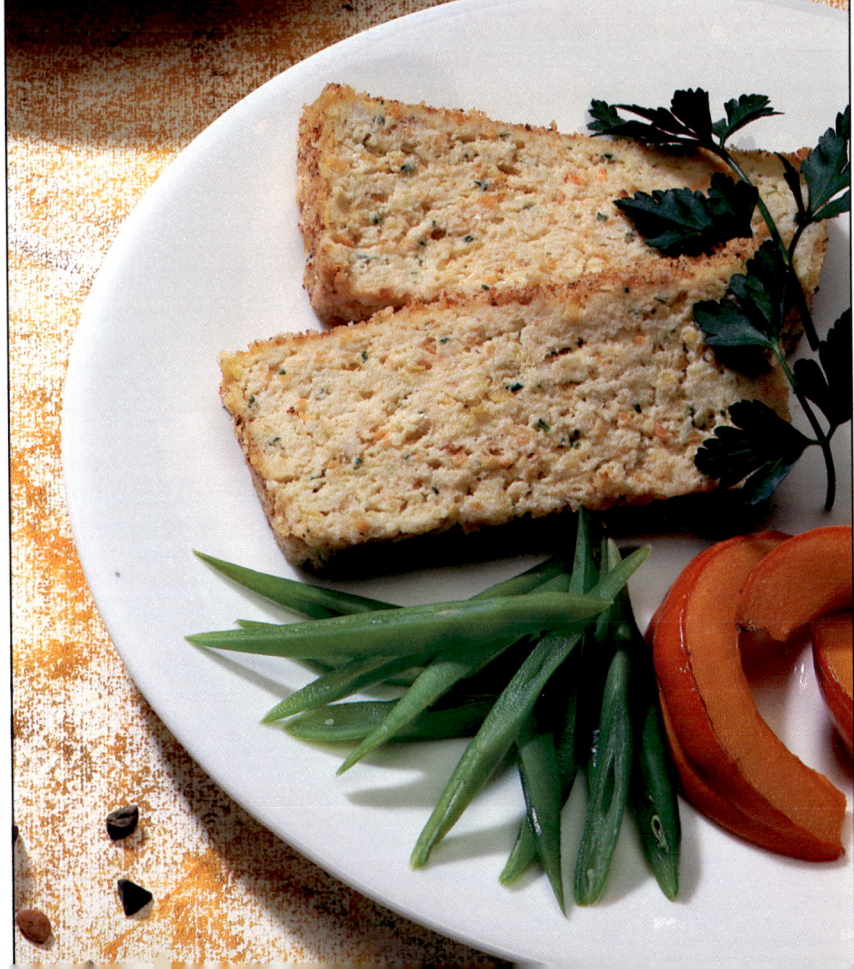

Roll up from short side, pinch ends to seal, place onto greased oven tray. Brush roll with remaining egg, sprinkle with cheese. Bake in hot oven for 10 minutes, reduce heat to moderate, bake further 20 minutes. Stand for 5 minutes before slicing. Serve with chunky tomato sauce.

Filling: Blend or process all ingredients until well combined.

Chunky Tomato Sauce: Heat oil in medium saucepan, add onion, garlic and pepper, stir constantly over heat until onion is soft. Add undrained crushed tomatoes and sugar, bring to boil, reduce heat, simmer, uncovered, for 5 minutes.

Blend cornflour with water, add to tomato mixture, stir over high heat until sauce boils and thickens.

Serves 6.

ABOVE: Herbed Fish Roll with Chunky Tomato Sauce. LEFT: Cucumber and Salmon Mould. RIGHT: Crunchy-Coated Fish Loaf.

PRAWN AND MUSHROOM OMELET

Filling is best prepared just before serving. Omelette must be cooked just before serving. Recipe unsuitable to freeze or microwave.

8 eggs
2 tablespoons water
30g butter
FILLING
30g butter
1 clove garlic, crushed
3 green shallots, chopped
125g baby mushrooms, sliced
500g cooked prawns, shelled
1 cup grated tasty cheese
1 tablespoon chopped fresh parsley
2 teaspoons light soy sauce

Make 1 omelette at a time. Break 2 of the eggs into small bowl, whisk in 2 teaspoons of the water. Heat 20cm heavy-based omelette pan over medium heat. Add quarter of the butter to hot pan, tilt pan to grease base and half-way up side.

Pour egg mixture into hot pan. Use spatula or egg slide to pull outside edges of setting egg mixture into centre of pan. When omelette is almost set, top with quarter of the filling, fold other half of omelette over filling, slide out onto hot serving plate. Repeat with remaining mixture.

Filling: Melt butter in small frying pan, add garlic, shallots and mushrooms, stir occasionally over medium heat until mushrooms are soft. Stir in prawns, cheese, parsley and sauce.

Makes 4.

DEEP-FRIED PRAWNS WITH SEASONED SALT

Prawns can be crumbed up to a day ahead; keep, covered, in refrigerator or freeze for up to 2 months. This recipe is not suitable to microwave.

1kg uncooked king prawns
plain flour
1 egg, lightly beaten
1 tablespoon milk
1 cup rolled oats
½ cup flaked almonds, chopped
oil for deep-frying
½ teaspoon five spice powder
2 teaspoons coarse cooking salt
CHIVE SAUCE
⅓ cup mayonnaise
⅓ cup sour cream
1 tablespoon chopped fresh chives
2 teaspoons lemon juice

Shell and devein prawns, leaving tails intact. Cut down backs, flatten slightly with hand. Dust prawns (except for tails) lightly with flour, dip in combined egg and milk. Press prawns into combined oats and almonds. Place in single layer on a plate, cover, refrigerate for 30 minutes.

Deep-fry prawns in hot oil a few at a time until golden brown. Remove from oil, drain on absorbent paper, sprinkle with combined five spice powder and salt. Serve with sauce.

Chive Sauce: Combine all ingredients in small bowl.

Serves 4 to 6.

FISH, PEPPER AND POTATO KEBABS

We used thick gemfish fillets in this recipe. Kebabs can be prepared a day ahead, keep, covered, in refrigerator. This recipe is not suitable to freeze or microwave.

½ cup lemon juice
¼ cup water
1 teaspoon sugar
1 clove garlic, crushed
1 tablespoon chopped fresh coriander
1 small fresh red chilli, finely chopped
750g white fish fillets
3 small zucchini, sliced
1 large red pepper, coarsely chopped
440g can potatoes, drained
1 teaspoon cornflour
1 tablespoon water, extra

Combine juice, water, sugar, garlic, coriander and chilli in large bowl. Mix in fish, zucchini, pepper and potatoes, stand for 2 hours.

Thread fish, zucchini, pepper and potatoes onto about 8 skewers; reserve lemon juice mixture. Grill or barbecue kebabs over medium heat for about 5 minutes on each side or until fish is tender.

Pour reserved lemon juice mixture into small saucepan, stir in cornflour blended with extra water. Stir constantly over high heat until mixture boils and thickens, serve spooned over kebabs.
Serves 4.

PRAWN, MANGO AND MACADAMIA SALAD

750g cooked king prawns
2 large mangoes, sliced
100g macadamia nuts
1 lettuce
LEMON BASIL DRESSING
¼ cup lemon juice
2 tablespoons oil
2 teaspoons chopped fresh basil
2 teaspoons castor sugar

Shell and devein prawns, leaving tails intact. Combine prawns, mangoes, nuts and lettuce in bowl, add dressing just before serving.
Lemon Basil Dressing: Combine all ingredients in jar; shake well.
Serves 4.

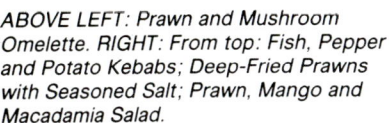

ABOVE LEFT: Prawn and Mushroom Omelette. RIGHT: From top: Fish, Pepper and Potato Kebabs; Deep-Fried Prawns with Seasoned Salt; Prawn, Mango and Macadamia Salad.

TUNA ASPARAGUS SALAD

Prepare salad just before serving. This recipe is not suitable to freeze.

- 1 small bunch fresh asparagus
- 2 x 185g cans chunk-style tuna in brine, drained
- 60g baby mushrooms
- 1 small red pepper, finely sliced
- 1 small long thin green cucumber, sliced
- 1 small lettuce
- 2 hard-boiled eggs, quartered

DRESSING
- 2 tablespoons white vinegar
- 1 cup oil
- 1 small red Spanish onion, finely chopped
- 1 clove garlic, chopped
- 3 green shallots, finely chopped

Boil, steam or microwave asparagus until tender, drain. Rinse under cold water, drain. Combine asparagus, tuna, mushrooms, pepper, cucumber, lettuce and eggs in medium bowl, add dressing just before serving.

Dressing: Combine vinegar, oil, onion, garlic and shallots in jar; shake well.

Serves 4.

BELOW: Clockwise from left: Cheesy Salmon Beignets; Pumpkin and Fish Roulade; Tuna Asparagus Salad. RIGHT: From left: Creamy Prawn Puff Cases; Spinach and Salmon Feta Rolls.

CHEESY SALMON BEIGNETS

Beignets are best served immediately they are made. This recipe is not suitable to freeze or microwave.

60g butter
1 medium onion, finely chopped
2 sticks celery, chopped
½ cup packaged breadcrumbs
¾ cup coarsely grated fresh parmesan cheese
1 cup water
75g butter, extra
1 cup plain flour
4 eggs, lightly beaten
210g can salmon, drained
oil for deep-frying

Melt half the butter in small frying pan, add onion and celery, stir constantly over medium heat until onion is soft (or microwave on HIGH for about 3 minutes), cool to room temperature.

Melt remaining butter in small saucepan, add breadcrumbs. Stir constantly over medium heat until breadcrumbs are lightly browned (or microwave on HIGH for about 2 minutes). Cool for 5 minutes, stir in half the cheese.

Combine water and extra butter in medium saucepan, stir constantly over heat until mixture boils and butter is melted. Add sifted flour all at once, stir vigorously over heat until mixture leaves side of saucepan and forms a smooth ball; remove from heat. Beat in eggs a little at a time, beating well after each addition (this can be done in an electric mixer or food processor). Stir in onion and celery mixture, flaked salmon and remaining cheese.

Deep-fry heaped tablespoons of mixture in hot oil, a few at a time, until golden brown. Remove beignets from oil, toss in breadcrumb mixture.

Makes about 16.

PUMPKIN AND FISH ROULADE

We used ling fillets for the filling. You will need to cook about 250g pumpkin for this recipe. Prepare roulade just before serving. Recipe unsuitable to freeze or microwave.

60g butter
⅓ cup plain flour
1 cup milk
1 cup mashed pumpkin
¼ teaspoon ground nutmeg
⅓ cup grated parmesan cheese
4 eggs, separated
FISH FILLING
500g white fish fillets
1 tablespoon mayonnaise
1 tablespoon thickened cream
2 tablespoons chopped fresh dill
1 tablespoon lemon juice

Grease 25cm x 30cm Swiss roll pan, line base and sides with greaseproof paper, grease paper. Melt butter in medium saucepan, add flour, stir constantly over heat for 1 minute. Remove from heat, gradually stir in milk, stir constantly over high heat until mixture boils and thickens. Stir in pumpkin, nutmeg, cheese and egg yolks, transfer mixture to large bowl.

Beat egg whites in small bowl with electric mixer until soft peaks form, fold lightly into pumpkin mixture. Spread mixture gently into prepared pan. Bake in hot oven for about 12 minutes or until puffed and golden brown.

Turn roulade onto clean tea-towel. Carefully remove lining paper, spread evenly with filling. Holding tea-towel with both hands, gently roll roulade from narrow end. Serve warm.

Fish Filling: Poach fish in simmering water until tender, drain, flake with fork. Combine fish in bowl with mayonnaise, cream, dill and lemon juice.

Serves 6.

CREAMY PRAWN PUFF CASES

Pastry cases can be cooked up to 2 days ahead; keep in airtight container. Serve as soon as they are filled. Recipe unsuitable to freeze or microwave.

1 sheet ready-rolled puff pastry
2 teaspoons milk
CREAMY PRAWN FILLING
60g butter
4 green shallots, chopped
2 tablespoons plain flour
⅔ cup cream
½ cup milk
¼ cup dry white wine
½ teaspoon grated lime rind
1 teaspoon lime juice
1kg cooked prawns, shelled

Cut pastry into 4 x 13cm rounds, cut 1cm slits around edges at 1cm intervals, brush edges with milk and fold edges over so they overlap, see picture. Place onto lightly greased oven tray, bake in moderately hot oven for about 10 minutes or until golden brown. Cut around edge of each puffed centre, remove each centre piece, add hot filling, replace each centre piece.

Creamy Prawn Filling: Melt butter in medium saucepan, add shallots, stir over heat for 1 minute. Add flour, stir constantly over heat for 1 minute. Remove from heat, gradually stir in combined cream, milk, wine, rind and juice, stir constantly over high heat until mixture boils and thickens; add prawns.

Serves 4.

SPINACH AND SALMON FETA ROLLS

Filling can be made up to a day ahead; rolls can be assembled ready for cooking several hours ahead; keep, covered, in refrigerator. This recipe is not suitable to freeze or microwave.

250g packet frozen spinach
100g feta cheese
125g packet cream cheese
440g can salmon, drained
2 tablespoons lemon juice
1 tablespoon mayonnaise
10 sheets fillo pastry
¼ cup oil, approximately

Press as much liquid as possible from thawed spinach. Blend or process cheeses, salmon, lemon juice and mayonnaise until smooth. Transfer to medium bowl, stir in spinach.

Brush each sheet of pastry with a little oil, layer 2 sheets together. Fold the 2 layered sheets in half, cut into 4 pieces. Repeat with remaining pastry.

Place about 2 level teaspoons of mixture across 1 corner of each piece of pastry, roll up, tucking in ends. Lightly brush rolls with oil, place on greased oven trays, bake in moderately hot oven for about 20 minutes or until lightly browned.

Makes 20.

PUMPKINS WITH PRAWNS IN COCONUT CREAM SAUCE

We used the flat-leafed Continental parsley in this recipe. Coconut sauce can be made up to 2 days ahead; keep, covered in refrigerator. Recipe unsuitable to freeze or microwave.

6 golden nugget pumpkins
15g butter
1 clove garlic, finely chopped
1 medium onion, finely chopped
1 teaspoon English mustard
2 tablespoons chopped fresh parsley
750g uncooked king prawns, shelled
COCONUT CREAM SAUCE
3 teaspoons butter
3 teaspoons plain flour
¼ cup milk
150g can coconut cream

Cut tops from pumpkins, reserve tops for lids. Trim base of each pumpkin to make level; scoop out seeds.

Heat butter in large frying pan, add garlic and onion, stir constantly over heat for about 3 minutes or until onion is soft. Stir in mustard, parsley and coconut cream sauce. Stir until combined; add prawns.

Divide prawn mixture evenly between pumpkins, replace tops of pumpkins. Place pumpkins in shallow baking dish, bake, uncovered, in moderate oven for about 45 minutes or until pumpkins are tender.

Coconut Cream Sauce: Melt butter in small saucepan, stir in flour, stir constantly over medium heat for 1 minute. Remove from heat, gradually stir in combined milk and coconut cream, stir constantly over high heat until mixture boils and thickens.

Serves 6.

SMOKED EEL AND LEEK QUICHE

Pastry case can be cooked up to a week in advance; keep in airtight container. Quiche is best cooked just before serving. This recipe is not suitable to freeze or microwave.

PASTRY
1¾ cups plain flour
155g butter
1 egg yolk
2 teaspoons lemon juice, approximately
FILLING
15g butter
1 small leek, sliced
250g smoked eel
3 eggs
300ml carton cream
½ cup milk
¾ cup grated tasty cheese
1 tablespoon chopped fresh chives
1 tablespoon chopped fresh parsley
1 teaspoon French mustard

Pastry: Sift flour into bowl; rub in butter. Add egg yolk and enough lemon juice to make ingredients cling together. Knead gently on lightly floured surface until smooth; cover, refrigerate for 30 minutes.

Roll pastry large enough to line deep 23cm flan tin. Lift pastry into flan tin, gently ease pastry into side of tin; trim edge of pastry. Place tin on oven tray, cover pastry with greaseproof or baking paper, fill with dried beans or rice. Bake in moderately hot oven for 7 minutes, remove paper and beans, bake pastry for further 7 minutes or until lightly browned. Cool to room temperature.

Place leek and eel into pastry case. Gently pour in egg mixture. Bake in moderate oven for about 35 minutes or until filling is set. Stand 5 minutes before serving.

Filling: Melt butter in small frying pan, add leek, cook over medium heat for about 5 minutes or until leek is soft; drain on absorbent paper, cool. Remove skin and bones from eel, flake flesh. Whisk eggs in large bowl, add cream, milk, cheese, herbs and mustard, whisk until just combined.

LEFT: From top: Pumpkins with Prawns in Coconut Cream Sauce; Smoked Eel and Leek Quiche. RIGHT: From top: Fish and Spinach Lasagne; Pasta with Mussels and Pine Nuts.

FISH AND SPINACH LASAGNE

We used gemfish fillets in this recipe. Lasagne can be prepared up to a day ahead or frozen for 2 months. Recipe unsuitable to microwave.

1 tablespoon oil
6 traditional lasagne sheets
250g packet frozen spinach, thawed
¾ cup grated tasty cheese
¼ cup grated parmesan cheese
MUSHROOM SAUCE
60g butter
500g white fish fillets, chopped
1 medium onion, chopped
1 clove garlic, crushed
125g mushrooms, sliced
½ teaspoon dried oregano leaves
425g can tomatoes
2 tablespoons tomato paste
CHEESE SAUCE
60g butter
⅓ cup plain flour
pinch nutmeg
2 cups milk
¼ cup grated parmesan cheese

Bring large saucepan of water to boil, add half the oil, gradually add lasagne sheets. Boil rapidly, uncovered, for about 10 minutes or until just tender; drain. Place cooked sheets into large bowl with cold water and remaining oil.

Place 2 of the lasagne sheets into ovenproof dish or 19cm x 29cm lamington pan. Spread with half the mushroom sauce, then half the cheese sauce. Press as much liquid as possible from spinach, spread spinach evenly over cheese sauce. Top with 2 more lasagne sheets, spread with remaining cheese sauce, top with remaining lasagne sheets.

Sprinkle with combined cheeses, bake in moderate oven for about 40 minutes or until golden brown. Stand for 10 minutes before serving.

Mushroom Sauce: Melt butter in large saucepan, add fish, stir gently over high heat for 2 minutes. Add onion, garlic and mushrooms, stir constantly over heat for about 3 minutes or until onion is soft. Add oregano, undrained crushed tomatoes and tomato paste to pan. Bring to boil, reduce heat, simmer, uncovered, for about 15 minutes or until sauce is thick; cool.

Cheese Sauce: Melt butter in medium saucepan, add flour and nutmeg, stir constantly over heat for 1 minute. Remove from heat, gradually stir in milk, stir constantly over high heat until sauce boils and thickens. Stir in cheese, cool.

Serves 6.

PASTA WITH MUSSELS AND PINE NUTS

We used tagliatelle in this recipe. Sauce can be made up to 4 days ahead or frozen for up to 2 months. Recipe unsuitable to microwave.

1kg mussels
250g pasta
2 teaspoons olive oil
TOMATO AND PINE NUT SAUCE
2 tablespoons olive oil
1 medium onion, finely chopped
1 clove garlic, crushed
⅓ cup pine nuts
410g can tomatoes
½ cup tomato purée
1 tablespoon chopped fresh oregano
12 pitted black olives

Cook mussels in large saucepan with about 1 cup water; remove mussel meat from shells. Cook pasta in large pan of boiling water until tender; drain, stir in oil. Combine mussels with sauce, serve with hot pasta.

Tomato and Pine Nut Sauce: Heat oil in medium saucepan, add onion and garlic, stir constantly over medium heat until onion is soft. Add pine nuts, stir constantly over medium heat until lightly browned. Stir in undrained crushed tomatoes and purée, bring to boil, reduce heat, simmer, uncovered, for about 5 minutes or until slightly thickened. Stir in oregano and olives just before serving.

Serves 4.

Plates & background: Villa Italiana

Background basket: Village Living

88

SEAFOOD VEGETABLE SPRING ROLLS

Rolls can be made 2 hours ahead, but are best fried just before serving. This recipe is unsuitable to freeze or microwave.

2 medium carrots
2 sticks celery
250g packet processed cheddar cheese
½ cup tomato sauce
8 seafood sticks
8 spring roll wrappers
2 teaspoons plain flour
1 tablespoon water
oil for deep-frying

Cut carrots, celery and cheese into strips the same length as the seafood sticks. Boil, steam or microwave carrots and celery until almost tender; drain. Rinse vegetables under cold water; drain, cool.

Place strips of carrot, celery and cheese with tomato sauce and a seafood stick diagonally across 1 end of each wrapper. Fold sides in, roll up firmly. Seal corner of pastry with a small amount of blended flour and water. Deep-fry rolls in hot oil for about a minute or until golden brown and crisp; drain on absorbent paper.

Makes 8.

ORIENTAL FISH AND VEGETABLE PUFFS

We used redfish fillets in this recipe. Puffs can be prepared for cooking up to a day ahead; keep, covered, in refrigerator. Recipe unsuitable to freeze or microwave.

250g white fish fillets
3 teaspoons oil
½ teaspoon sesame oil
1 clove garlic, crushed
1 stick celery, finely chopped
1 small red pepper, finely chopped
1 cup bean sprouts, chopped
3 green shallots, finely chopped
1 tablespoon oyster sauce
1 small fresh red chilli, finely chopped
3 teaspoons chopped fresh basil
375g packet frozen puff pastry, thawed
oil for deep-frying

Blend or process fish until smooth, transfer to medium bowl. Heat both oils in frying pan, add garlic, celery and pepper, stir constantly over medium heat until celery is almost tender; cool.

Add celery mixture, sprouts, shallots, sauce, chilli and basil to fish, mix well. Cover, refrigerate for 30 minutes. Roll out half the pastry to 24cm × 35cm rectangle. Cut into 6 rounds using 11cm cutter.

Place a heaped tablespoon of mixture onto each round, fold in half to enclose filling, roll and fold edges. Deep-fry puffs about 4 at a time in hot oil for about a minute or until golden brown and cooked through; drain on absorbent paper.

Makes 12.

KOKODA

This delicious recipe from Fiji contains uncooked fish; the marinating changes the texture so it tastes cooked. We used mullet fillets for this recipe. Fish can be marinated up to a day ahead; keep, covered in refrigerator. This recipe is not suitable to freeze.

750g oily fish fillets, chopped
1 teaspoon salt
¼ cup white vinegar
½ cup lemon juice
1 medium green pepper, chopped
150g can coconut cream
½ × 250g punnet cherry tomatoes, halved
2 tablespoons chopped fresh chives
1 small fresh red chilli, finely chopped
1 teaspoon sugar

Combine fish, salt, vinegar and juice in large bowl, cover, refrigerate for about 3 hours or overnight. Transfer fish to large strainer or colander. Rinse fish under cold water until water runs clear; drain. Combine fish, pepper, cream, tomatoes, chives, chilli and sugar in large bowl; refrigerate mixture until serving time.

Serves 4.

SMOKED TROUT SALAD IN PITA POCKETS

Trout mixture can be prepared several hours before filling into pockets; keep, covered, in refrigerator. This recipe is not suitable to freeze.

350g smoked trout
½ small lettuce, shredded
1 punnet alfalfa sprouts
1 medium carrot, grated
3 green shallots, finely chopped
6 bottled artichokes, chopped
6 small pita pocket breads
¼ cup mayonnaise

Remove skin and bones from trout; flake flesh. Combine trout, lettuce, sprouts, carrot, shallots and artichokes in large bowl. Cut pocket breads in half, spread inside pockets with mayonnaise, fill with trout mixture.

Makes 6.

Bowls: African Heritage

ABOVE: From top: Smoked Trout Salad in Pita Pockets; Kokoda. LEFT: From top: Oriental Fish and Vegetable Puffs; Seafood Vegetable Spring Rolls.

MINI STEAMED BUNS WITH SEAFOOD SAUCE

We used flathead fillets in this recipe. Cook buns just before serving. Sauce can be made a day ahead. Recipe unsuitable to freeze or microwave.

STEAMED BUNS
15g dry yeast
1¼ cups warm water
½ cup castor sugar
2 cups plain flour
1 cup self-raising flour
30g lard, melted
SEAFOOD SAUCE
6 Chinese dried mushrooms
60g butter
1 clove garlic, crushed
1 teaspoon grated fresh ginger
3 green shallots, chopped
1 stick celery, chopped
6 white fish fillets, chopped
200g cooked shelled prawns, chopped
3 teaspoons cornflour
⅓ cup oyster sauce
¾ cup water
1 small chicken stock cube, crumbled

Combine yeast, one-third cup of the water and 2 teaspoons of the sugar in small bowl. Sprinkle with 2 teaspoons of the plain flour. Cover, stand in warm place 10 minutes or until frothy. Combine remaining sugar and remaining sifted flours in large bowl, make well in centre, stir in remaining water, lard and yeast mixture; mix to a soft dough. Turn dough onto floured surface, knead well for 10 minutes or until dough is smooth and elastic. Place in lightly oiled bowl, cover, stand in warm place for about 1 hour or until dough is doubled in bulk.

Repeat kneading and rising again. Knead dough until smooth, divide into 36 pieces. Knead each piece into ball, place onto 7cm square of greaseproof paper. Place buns on paper 5cm apart in steamer, cover, steam over boiling water for about 10 minutes or until buns are dry to touch. Remove paper, serve with sauce.

Seafood Sauce: Cover mushrooms with boiling water, stand 20 minutes. Drain mushrooms, remove and discard stems, chop caps finely. Melt butter in large frying pan or wok, add garlic, ginger and shallots, stir-fry 2 minutes. Add celery, mushrooms, fish and prawns, stir-fry 2 minutes. Add cornflour blended oyster sauce, water and stock cube, add to pan, stir-fry until mixture boils and thickens.

Makes 36.

SCALLOPS WITH CHINESE VEGETABLES

This dish must be served as soon as it is cooked. This recipe is unsuitable to freeze or microwave.

1 tablespoon oil
¼ teaspoon sesame oil
1 clove garlic, crushed
1 teaspoon grated fresh ginger
1 medium onion, sliced
1 small red pepper, sliced
200g broccoli, chopped
500g scallops
1 tablespoon oyster sauce
1 tablespoon light soy sauce
½ small chicken stock cube, crumbled
2 teaspoons cornflour
½ cup water

Heat both oils in wok or frying pan, add garlic and ginger, stir-fry over medium heat for 30 seconds. Add onion, pepper and broccoli, stir-fry over high heat for 2 minutes. Add scallops, sauces, stock cube and cornflour blended with water. Stir-fry over high heat until mixture boils and thickens. Serve with boiled rice, if desired.

Serves 4.

SEAFOOD IN TEMPURA BATTER

We used ling fillets in this dish. Recipe unsuitable to freeze or microwave.

500g white fish fillets
500g uncooked king prawns
200g broccoli, chopped
3 small zucchini, sliced
2 medium onions, sliced
oil for deep-frying
TEMPURA BATTER
1 egg
½ cup cornflour
½ cup plain flour
¾ cup water
DIPPING SAUCE
¼ cup light soy sauce
¼ cup water
1 small fresh red chilli, finely chopped
1 clove garlic, crushed
1 tablespoon chopped fresh coriander

Cut fish into 1cm strips. Shell prawns, leaving tails intact; cut down backs, flatten prawns slightly with hand. Boil, steam or microwave broccoli and zucchini until just tender; drain, pat dry with absorbent paper.

Dip fish, prawns, broccoli, zucchini and onion rings into batter. Deep-fry pieces a few at a time in hot oil until lightly browned, drain on absorbent paper; serve hot with sauce.

Tempura Batter: Beat egg in small bowl with electric mixer until thick and creamy, fold in sifted flours and water in 2 batches, stir until smooth.

Dipping Sauce: Combine all ingredients in small bowl.

Serves 4.

ABOVE: From left: Seafood in Tempura Batter; Mini Steamed Buns with Seafood Sauce; Scallops with Chinese Vegetables. ABOVE RIGHT: Salmon and Corn Muffins with Cheese Spread. BELOW RIGHT: Trout Soufflé.

SALMON AND CORN MUFFINS WITH CHEESE SPREAD

Muffins are best eaten hot from the oven but can be frozen for 2 months. Recipe unsuitable to microwave.

210g can salmon, drained
130g can creamed corn
¼ cup chopped fresh parsley
½ small red pepper, finely chopped
2 cups self-raising flour
45g butter
½ cup milk
¼ cup buttermilk
1 egg, lightly beaten
½ cup grated tasty cheese
CHEESE SPREAD
125g tub soft cream cheese
1 tablespoon cream
1 teaspoon lemon juice
2 tablespoons chopped fresh chives

Lightly grease large deep muffin pans (⅓ cup capacity). Combine flaked salmon, corn, parsley and pepper in small bowl. Sift flour into medium bowl, rub in butter, stir in combined milks and egg, stir until combined. Stir in salmon mixture. Spoon mixture into prepared pans, sprinkle with cheese, bake in moderately hot oven for about 30 minutes. Serve with cheese spread.
Cheese Spread: Combine all ingredients in small bowl.
Makes 12.

TROUT SOUFFLE

Soufflé must be served immediately it is cooked. Recipe unsuitable to freeze.

30g butter
4 trout fillets
60g butter, extra
¼ cup plain flour
1½ cups milk
2 tablespoons chopped fresh chives
4 eggs, separated

Melt butter in large frying pan. Add fish, cook for 3 minutes each side (or microwave on MEDIUM HIGH for about 2 minutes each side) or until tender. Remove fish from pan, remove skin and bones, flake fish; cool.

Melt extra butter in large saucepan, stir in flour, stir constantly over heat for 3 minutes (or microwave on HIGH for about 2 minutes). Remove from heat, gradually stir in milk, return to heat, stir constantly over high heat (or microwave on HIGH for about 5 minutes) until mixture boils and thickens; cool. Stir in chives, fish and egg yolks.

Beat egg whites in small bowl with electric mixer until firm peaks form. Fold egg whites into sauce mixture. Pour mixture into soufflé dish (8 cup capacity). Bake in moderately hot oven for about 45 minutes or until firm.
Serves 4.

SMOKED FISH CROQUETTES

We used haddock in this recipe. Croquette mixture can be prepared up to a day ahead; keep, covered, in refrigerator. This recipe is not suitable to freeze or microwave.

500g smoked fish
30g butter
1 cup short grain rice
3½ cups water
1 tablespoon lemon juice
2 cups (250g) grated mozzarella cheese
1 small chicken stock cube, crumbled
2 eggs, lightly beaten
2 eggs, lightly beaten, extra
2 tablespoons water, extra
2 cups packaged breadcrumbs
oil for deep-frying

Place fish in large frying pan, barely cover with cold water. Bring to boil, drain, repeat this process; drain well, flake fish.

Melt butter in large saucepan, add rice, mix well, add the 3½ cups water, cover, bring to boil over high heat. Reduce heat to as low as possible, cook for about 30 minutes or until all water is absorbed. Stir in juice, cheese, stock cube, eggs and fish.

Spread mixture onto tray covered with plastic wrap, refrigerate for about 1 hour or until mixture is firm enough to handle. Shape mixture into 20 croquettes, dip into combined extra eggs and extra water, toss in breadcrumbs. Deep-fry croquettes in hot oil a few at a time until golden brown; drain on absorbent paper.

Makes 20.

FISH AND BACON PIE

We used ling fillets in this recipe. Filling can be prepared up to 4 hours ahead; cook pie just before serving. Recipe unsuitable to freeze or microwave.

1kg white fish fillets
30g butter
2 medium onions, chopped
2 bacon rashers, chopped
2 x 425g cans tomatoes
½ cup water
1 tablespoon tomato paste
1 teaspoon sugar
1 cup frozen peas
1 tablespoon cornflour
2 tablespoons water, extra
375g packet frozen puff pastry, thawed
1 egg yolk, lightly beaten

Poach fish in large frying pan of simmering water, simmer for about 5 minutes or until just tender; drain, cool, flake.

Heat butter in a large frying pan, add onions and bacon, stir constantly over medium heat for about 3 minutes or until onions are soft. Add undrained crushed tomatoes, water, tomato paste and sugar. Bring to boil, reduce heat, simmer, uncovered, for about 40 minutes or until mixture is thick and pulpy. Stir in peas and cornflour blended with extra water; stir constantly over high heat until mixture boils and thickens; cool. Spread mixture into deep 22cm pie plate.

Roll pastry on lightly floured surface large enough to cover mixture in pie plate, decorate with remaining pastry scraps, if desired. Brush pie with egg yolk, bake in moderately hot oven for about 25 minutes or until brown.

BELOW: Clockwise from left: Potato and Salmon Salad; Fish and Bacon Pie; Smoked Fish Croquettes. RIGHT: Fish and Spinach Cannelloni.

POTATO AND SALMON SALAD

Salad without lettuce can be prepared up to a day ahead. This recipe is not suitable to freeze.

**3 medium potatoes, chopped
1 medium apple, chopped
3 sticks celery, chopped
½ cup walnut pieces
4 green shallots, chopped
440g can salmon, drained
¾ cup mayonnaise
¼ cup cream
1 tablespoon lime juice
1 medium lettuce**

Boil, steam or microwave potatoes until tender; drain, cool. Combine potatoes, apple, celery, walnuts, shallots and flaked salmon in large bowl. Gently stir in combined mayonnaise, cream and lime juice. Serve in lettuce-lined bowl.

Serves 4.

FISH AND SPINACH CANNELLONI

We used ling fillets in this recipe. Cannelloni can be frozen for 2 months. Recipe unsuitable to microwave.

**250g packet frozen spinach, thawed
15g butter
1 small onion, finely chopped
1½ tablespoons plain flour
1½ cups milk
375g white fish fillets, finely chopped
130g packet cannelloni tubes
½ cup grated tasty cheese
2 tablespoons grated fresh parmesan cheese**
TOMATO SAUCE
**1 teaspoon oil
1 clove garlic, crushed
1 small onion, finely chopped
1½ cups bottled spaghetti sauce
2 teaspoons chopped fresh basil
½ teaspoon castor sugar**

Press as much liquid as possible from spinach. Melt butter in medium saucepan, add onion, cook for 2 minutes or until onion is soft. Add flour, stir constantly over heat for 1 minute. Remove from heat, gradually stir in milk, stir constantly over high heat until mixture boils and thickens. Reduce heat, add fish and spinach, simmer 10 minutes, cool.

Place mixture into large piping bag without a tube, pipe mixture into cannelloni tubes, place in single layer in greased ovenproof dish (8 cup capacity). Pour tomato sauce over cannelloni, sprinkle with combined cheeses. Bake in moderate oven for about 40 minutes or until brown.

Tomato Sauce: Heat oil in medium saucepan, add garlic and onion, stir over medium heat for about 2 minutes or until onion is soft. Add sauce, basil and sugar, bring to boil, reduce heat, simmer, uncovered for about 5 minutes or until slightly thickened.

Serves 4.

SEAFOOD AND PASTA ITALIANA

We used penne pasta in this recipe; cook 1 cup to give the 2½ cups required. We used gemfish fillets. This dish can be prepared up to a day ahead; keep, covered, in refrigerator or freeze for up to 2 months. The recipe is not suitable to microwave.

500g thick white fish fillets, chopped
2 tablespoons plain flour
¼ cup oil
1 medium onion, finely chopped
1 clove garlic, crushed
410g can tomatoes
130g can diced capsicum, drained
2 tablespoons tomato paste
¼ cup water
8 pitted green olives
2 teaspoons drained capers, chopped
50g can anchovy fillets, drained, chopped
1 small fresh red chilli, finely chopped
2½ cups cooked pasta

Combine fish and flour in plastic bag, toss until fish is well coated; remove from bag, shake off excess flour. Heat 2 tablespoons of the oil in large frying pan, add fish, cook over medium heat until fish is tender. Remove fish from pan, drain on absorbent paper.

Heat remaining oil in pan, add onion and garlic, stir over heat for about 2 minutes or until onion is soft. Add the undrained crushed tomatoes, capsicum, tomato paste, water, olives, capers, anchovies and chilli. Bring to boil, reduce heat, simmer, uncovered, for about 15 minutes or until mixture is thick. Add fish and pasta, stir gently over medium heat until combined and heated through.
Serves 4.

CRUMBED SQUID WITH TOMATO SAUCE

Squid are best cooked just before serving. This recipe is not suitable to microwave.

500g squid hoods
plain flour
2 eggs, lightly beaten
2 tablespoons milk
2 cups (250g) packaged breadcrumbs
oil for deep-frying
TOMATO SAUCE
2 tablespoons oil
2 cloves garlic, crushed
1 medium onion, finely chopped
2 tablespoons tomato paste
410g can tomatoes
3 teaspoons cornflour
¼ cup water

Cut squid hoods into rings. Toss lightly in flour. Dip rings into combined eggs and milk, toss in breadcrumbs. Deep-fry in hot oil for about 30 seconds or until golden brown and tender, serve with sauce.

Tomato Sauce: Heat oil in frying pan, add garlic and onion, stir over medium heat for about 2 minutes or until onion is soft. Add paste, undrained crushed tomatoes and cornflour blended with water. Stir constantly over high heat until mixture boils and thickens. Blend or purée to dipping consistency.
Serves 4.

CRAB NACHOS

Crab and bean mixture can be made a day ahead; keep, covered, in refrigerator. This recipe is not suitable to freeze or microwave.

2 x 170g cans crab, drained
310g can red kidney beans, drained
410g can tomatoes, drained
2 tablespoons tomato paste
½ x 35g packet taco seasoning mix
100g packaged corn chips
1½ cups (185g) grated tasty cheese
1 medium avocado
1 tablespoon lemon juice
½ cup sour cream

Combine crab, beans, crushed tomatoes, tomato paste and seasoning in large saucepan. Bring to boil, reduce heat, simmer, uncovered, for about 10 minutes or until mixture is thick; stir occasionally.

Pour mixture into large ovenproof dish, top with corn chips, sprinkle with cheese. Bake in moderate oven for about 15 minutes or until cheese is melted. Blend or process avocado and lemon juice until smooth. Serve nachos topped with avocado mixture and sour cream.
Serves 6.

BELOW: Crab Nachos. LEFT: From top: Crumbed Squid with Tomato Sauce; Seafood and Pasta Italiana.

CRAB AND CORN PANCAKES WITH SPICY YOGHURT SALAD

Pancake mixture and salad can be prepared several hours ahead; keep, covered, in refrigerator. This recipe is not suitable to freeze or microwave.

**170g can crab, drained
2 small potatoes, finely grated
1 medium carrot, finely grated
130g can creamed corn
130g can corn kernels, drained
3 green shallots, finely chopped
1 tablespoon chopped fresh parsley
1 egg, lightly beaten
2 tablespoons sour cream
2 tablespoons oil
SPICY YOGHURT SALAD
3 medium carrots, coarsely grated
1 tablespoon chopped fresh parsley
3 teaspoons chilli sauce
¾ cup plain yoghurt
2 teaspoons honey**

Press excess liquid from crab, potatoes and carrot. Combine crab, potatoes, carrot, both cans of corn, shallots, parsley, egg and cream in large bowl.

Heat oil in large frying pan, pour ¼ cup mixture into pan, flatten gently with egg slide, cook over medium heat for about 5 minutes on each side or until crisp; turn cakes once during cooking; drain on absorbent paper. Serve with spicy yoghurt salad.

Spicy Yoghurt Salad: Press excess liquid from carrots. Combine carrots, parsley, sauce, yoghurt and honey in medium bowl.

Serves 4.

LEMON FISH FINGER TOASTIES

We used ocean perch in this recipe. Toasties can be prepared several hours ahead of cooking; keep, covered, in refrigerator. Cook just before serving. This recipe is not suitable to freeze or microwave.

**250g white fish fillets
1 teaspoon grated lemon rind
¼ teaspoon dried thyme leaves
2 teaspoons cornflour
1 egg white
6 slices wholemeal bread
½ cup packaged ground almonds
oil for deep-frying**

Blend or process fish until smooth, place in medium bowl. Mix in rind, thyme, cornflour and egg white. Remove crusts from bread, spread fish mixture over 1 side of each slice, dip bread with fish-side-down into almonds. Deep-fry toasties in hot oil until golden brown, drain on absorbent paper. Cut each slice into 3 fingers.

Makes 18.

GRILLED FISH WITH FRESH HERB BUTTER

We used ocean perch in this recipe. Herb butter can be frozen for 2 months. Recipe unsuitable to microwave.

**4 thick white fish fillets
15g butter, melted
HERB BUTTER
125g butter
2 tablespoons lemon juice
1 teaspoon chopped fresh thyme
2 teaspoons chopped fresh watercress
½ teaspoon chopped fresh rosemary
1 tablespoon chopped fresh parsley**

Place fish on lightly greased oven tray, brush lightly with butter, grill for about 7 minutes or until fish is tender. Serve topped with herb butter.

Herb Butter: Beat butter in small bowl with electric mixer until creamy. Beat in juice and herbs. Shape butter into log, wrap in foil, freeze until firm.

Serves 4.

LEFT: From top: Lemon Fish Finger Toasties; Grilled Fish with Fresh Herb Butter. RIGHT: Crab and Corn Pancakes with Spicy Yoghurt Salad.

GNOCCHI WITH SEAFOOD SAUCE

For best results use old, dry, firm-textured potatoes. Gnocchi can be frozen for up to 3 months; cook gnocchi while still frozen. Sauce is best served as soon as it is made; it is unsuitable to freeze. This recipe is not suitable to microwave.

GNOCCHI
500g potatoes
125g ricotta cheese
1 tablespoon chopped fresh parsley
½ cup plain flour

SEAFOOD SAUCE
30g butter
⅓ cup plain flour
2 cups water
1 small chicken stock cube, crumbled
2 teaspoons tomato paste
1 tablespoon dry red wine
2 tablespoons cream
¼ teaspoon dried thyme leaves
1 tablespoon chopped fresh parsley
500g cooked prawns, shelled
250g scallops
125g cooked mussel meat

Gnocchi: Boil, steam or microwave potatoes until tender, drain, press through sieve; cool to room temperature. using hand, knead ricotta cheese and parsley into potato in large bowl, then work in sifted flour; do this in several batches.

Turn dough onto lightly floured surface, knead until smooth, divide mixture into 4 pieces. Roll each quarter into log shape about 2cm diameter. Cut logs into 4cm pieces, roll into balls. Press the floured prongs of a fork into top of mixture to make indentations.

Bring large saucepan of water to boil, add half the gnocchi, reduce heat, simmer for about 5 minutes or until gnocchi float to the top. Remove with slotted spoon, keep warm. Repeat with remaining gnocchi. Serve with sauce.

Seafood Sauce: Melt butter in medium saucepan, stir in flour; stir constantly over heat for 1 minute. Remove from heat, gradually stir in water, stock cube, paste and wine. Return to heat, stir constantly over high heat until mixture boils and thickens, stir in cream, thyme, parsley and seafood, cook without boiling until seafood is heated through.

Serves 4.

TUNA AND SESAME SNACKS

Snacks can be prepared up to 2 hours before cooking; serve as soon as they are cooked. This recipe is not suitable to freeze or microwave.

3 medium potatoes, chopped
2 x 185g cans tuna in brine, drained
1 egg yolk
4 green shallots, chopped
1 stick celery, chopped
plain flour
1 egg, lightly beaten
1 tablespoon milk
¼ cup packaged breadcrumbs
¼ cup sesame seeds
oil for deep-frying

Boil, steam or microwave potatoes until tender; drain. Place in large bowl, mash, cool for 5 minutes. Stir in tuna, egg yolk, shallots and celery; cover, refrigerate for 15 minutes.

Roll heaped teaspoons of mixture into balls with lightly floured hands, dip into combined egg and milk, then into combined breadcrumbs and sesame seeds. Deep-fry balls a few at a time in hot oil until golden brown, drain on absorbent paper.

Makes about 36.

PRAWN AND RICE FRITTERS

You will need to cook ⅓ cup rice for the fritters. This recipe is not suitable to freeze or microwave.

¾ cup self-raising flour
1 cup cooked rice
1 egg, lightly beaten
1 cup milk
2 green shallots, chopped
500g cooked medium prawns, shelled
2 tablespoons oil, approximately

Sift flour into medium bowl, add rice, make well in centre, stir in combined egg and milk, shallots and prawns.

Heat half the oil in large frying pan, drop heaped tablespoons of mixture into pan. Cook fritters on both sides until golden brown, drain on absorbent paper. Repeat with remaining oil and prawn mixture. Add more oil during cooking, if necessary.

Makes about 15.

Bowl, shell plate & spoon: Village Living

RIGHT: From top: Tuna and Sesame Snacks; Prawn and Rice Fritters. LEFT: Gnocchi with Seafood Sauce.

Plates: Clay Things

FOR THE BARBECUE

Seafood of all kind is wonderful for the barbecue as it is easy to prepare and cooks quickly. A bonus is the sizzling good flavour it gets from this open style of cooking – flavour enhanced by specially tasty glazes, sauces and accompaniments. If you prefer, you can grill or pan-fry many recipes with delicious results.

SKEWERED MUSSELS WITH SPICY HONEY GLAZE

Mussels can be wrapped in bacon, threaded onto skewers and marinated in glaze several hours ahead; keep, covered, in refrigerator. This recipe is not suitable to freeze or microwave.

1kg mussels
8 bacon rashers
SPICY HONEY GLAZE
2 tablespoons honey
2 tablespoons tomato sauce
1 teaspoon Worcestershire sauce
¼ teaspoon tabasco sauce

Cook mussels in large saucepan of water, remove mussels from shells. Cut bacon into 2cm x 6cm strips. Wrap mussels in bacon, thread onto skewers. Place skewers in single layer in dish, top with glaze. Marinate in refrigerator for about 1 hour.

Remove from glaze, barbecue or grill until bacon is crisp and mussels tender. Brush occasionally with remaining glaze during cooking.
Spicy Honey Glaze: Combine honey and sauces in small bowl.

Serves 4.

Clockwise from left: Skewered Mussels with Spicy Honey Glaze; Green Peppercorn and Lemon Fish Cutlets; Fish Cakes with Cucumber and Mint Chutney.

FISH CAKES WITH CUCUMBER AND MINT CHUTNEY

We used redfish fillets for this recipe. Cakes can be made up to a day ahead; keep, covered, in refrigerator or freeze for up to a month. Chutney is best made just before serving. This recipe is not suitable to microwave.

1 small carrot, finely grated
375g white fish fillets
1 tablespoon fish sauce
2 teaspoons sugar
2 teaspoons chopped fresh coriander
1 teaspoon paprika
1 teaspoon grated lime rind
2 cloves garlic, crushed
2 teaspoons grated fresh ginger
3 green shallots, chopped
125g green beans, chopped
plain flour
2 tablespoons oil, approximately
CUCUMBER AND MINT CHUTNEY
⅓ cup white vinegar
1 tablespoon sugar
1 small cucumber, finely chopped
1 small red pepper, chopped
1 tablespoon chopped fresh mint
1 tablespoon lime juice
1 small onion, sliced

Squeeze moisture from carrot. Blend or process fish, sauce, sugar, coriander, paprika, rind, garlic, ginger and shallots until combined. Transfer mixture to large bowl, mix in carrot and beans.

Divide mixture into 8 patties. Toss in flour, shake away excess flour, brush cakes on both sides with a little oil. Barbecue, grill or pan-fry for about 3 minutes on each side or until patties are browned and cooked through.
Cucumber and Mint Chutney: Combine vinegar and sugar in small bowl, stir until sugar is dissolved. Add cucumber, pepper, mint, juice and onion; mix well.

Makes 8.

GREEN PEPPERCORN AND LEMON FISH CUTLETS

We used jewfish cutlets in this recipe. Fish can be prepared for cooking up to a day ahead; keep, covered, in refrigerator. This recipe is not suitable to freeze or microwave.

4 white fish cutlets
½ cup lemon juice
2 tablespoons canned drained green peppercorns
1 tablespoon chopped fresh thyme
2 green shallots, chopped

Combine fish, juice, peppercorns, thyme and shallots in shallow dish, cover, refrigerate several hours or overnight. Cook on well-greased hot plate or in frying pan for about 10 minutes or until tender. Brush fish with marinade during cooking.

Serves 4.

FISH BURGERS

We used thick ling fillets in this recipe. Patties can be prepared for cooking up to a day ahead, keep, covered, in refrigerator. They can be frozen for up to 2 months.

750g white fish fillets
¾ cup stale breadcrumbs
¼ cup chopped fresh parsley
1 egg
plain flour
6 hamburger buns
6 lettuce leaves
alfalfa sprouts
1 medium tomato, sliced
CHEESE AND HERB FILLING
½ cup grated tasty cheese
1 tablespoon chopped fresh parsley
1 tablespoon chopped fresh chives
GARLIC MAYONNAISE
½ cup mayonnaise
1 clove garlic, crushed
1 tablespoon chopped fresh chives

Blend or process fish, breadcrumbs, parsley and egg until smooth. Divide mixture into 6 portions. Press a level tablespoon of filling into centre of each portion. Shape mixture around filling to form patties.

Toss each patty lightly in flour, cook on well-greased barbecue plate or in frying pan for about 5 minutes on each side (or microwave on MEDIUM HIGH for about 3 minutes each side) or until cooked through.

Split buns, toast cut sides under hot griller. Make burgers, using patties, lettuce, sprouts and tomato, and top with garlic mayonnaise.
Cheese and Herb Filling: Combine all ingredients in small bowl.
Garlic Mayonnaise: Combine all ingredients in small bowl.
Makes 6.

SKEWERED GARFISH ROLLS

Prepare garfish the same way as sardines, see glossary. Rolls can be prepared for cooking up to a day ahead; keep, covered, in refrigerator. This recipe is not suitable to freeze or microwave.

8 medium garfish
30g butter, softened
2 teaspoons seeded mustard
1 clove garlic, crushed
4 green shallots
2 tablespoons oil
plain flour

Remove heads and backbones from garfish. Combine butter, mustard and garlic in small bowl, spread evenly over inside of fish. Cut shallots into 5cm strips, place a few strips of shallot at head end and gently but firmly roll garfish towards tail. Repeat making rolls with remaining fish, butter mixture and shallots.

Place 2 rolls on each skewer. Heat oil on hot plate, lightly dust fish rolls with flour, cook on hot plate or in frying pan for about 10 minutes or until fish are tender.
Serves 4.

FISH WITH SPICY SEASONING

We used mullet in this recipe. You will need to cook ⅓ cup of rice for seasoning. Fish can be prepared for cooking up to a day ahead; keep, covered, in refrigerator. Uncooked fish can be frozen for up to 2 months.

4 whole oily fish
2 tablespoons oil
1 small onion, chopped
1 small fresh red chilli, chopped
2 teaspoons chopped fresh coriander
1 teaspoon garam masala
½ teaspoon ground cumin
1 small green pepper, chopped
1 cup cooked rice
1 egg, lightly beaten

Remove heads and backbones from fish, leaving fillets joined.

Heat oil in large frying pan, add onion, chilli, coriander, garam masala and cumin, stir constantly over medium heat for about 2 minutes (or microwave on HIGH for about 3 minutes) or until onion is soft.

Add pepper and rice to pan, stir constantly over medium heat for 3 minutes (or microwave on HIGH for about 1 minute); cool mixture to room temperature. Stir egg into rice mixture, fill cavity of fish with this seasoning.

Tie string around fish at 3cm intervals. Cook fish on well-greased hot plate or in frying pan; cook with seasoning-side-down first. Cook for about 5 minutes each side (or microwave on MEDIUM HIGH for about 4 minutes on each side) or until fish is cooked through. Remove string, stand few minutes before slicing.

Serves 4.

ABOVE: From left: Skewered Garfish Rolls; Fish with Spicy Seasoning. LEFT: Fish Burgers.

BALMAIN BUGS WITH LIME BUTTER

These are best prepared just before serving. This recipe is not suitable to freeze or microwave.

8 large uncooked Balmain bugs
60g butter, melted
¼ cup lime juice
1 clove garlic, finely chopped
1 tablespoon chopped fresh dill
¼ teaspoon ground black pepper

Cut soft shell covering away from underside of Balmain bugs. Brush with combined butter, lime juice, garlic, dill and pepper, barbecue or grill Balmain bugs until tender, brushing with butter mixture during cooking.

Serves 4.

Plate: Country Floors; spice drawers: Appley Hoare Antiques.

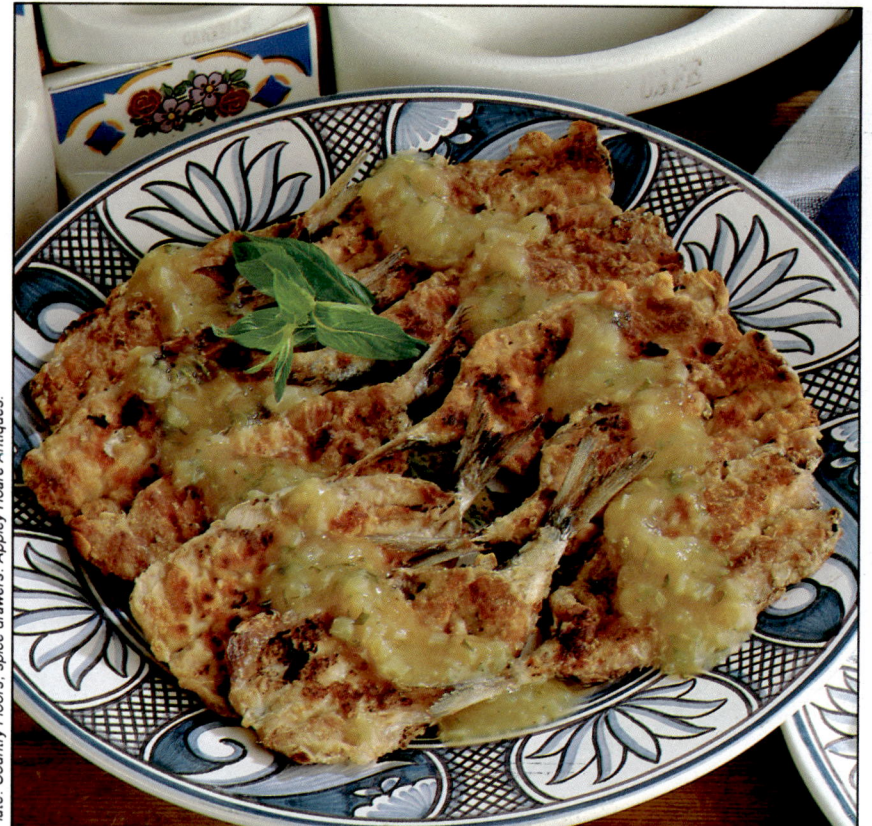

MARINATED SQUID AND WATER CHESTNUT KEBABS

Kebabs can be prepared ready for cooking a day ahead; keep, covered, in refrigerator. This recipe is not suitable to freeze or microwave.

500g squid hoods
2 tablespoons tomato paste
¼ cup brown sugar
2 tablespoons red wine vinegar
¼ cup teriyaki marinade
1 teaspoon grated fresh ginger
2 cloves garlic, crushed
2 teaspoons sesame seeds
410g can water chestnuts, drained

Cut squid hoods open, cut diamond pattern on the inside; do not cut through. Cut squid into strips. Combine squid, tomato paste, brown sugar, vinegar, marinade, ginger, garlic and sesame seeds in large bowl, cover, refrigerate several hours or overnight. Weave squid strips around chestnuts when threading onto skewers; use about 3 chestnuts per skewer. Barbecue or grill for about 5 minutes or until squid are tender.

Serves 4.

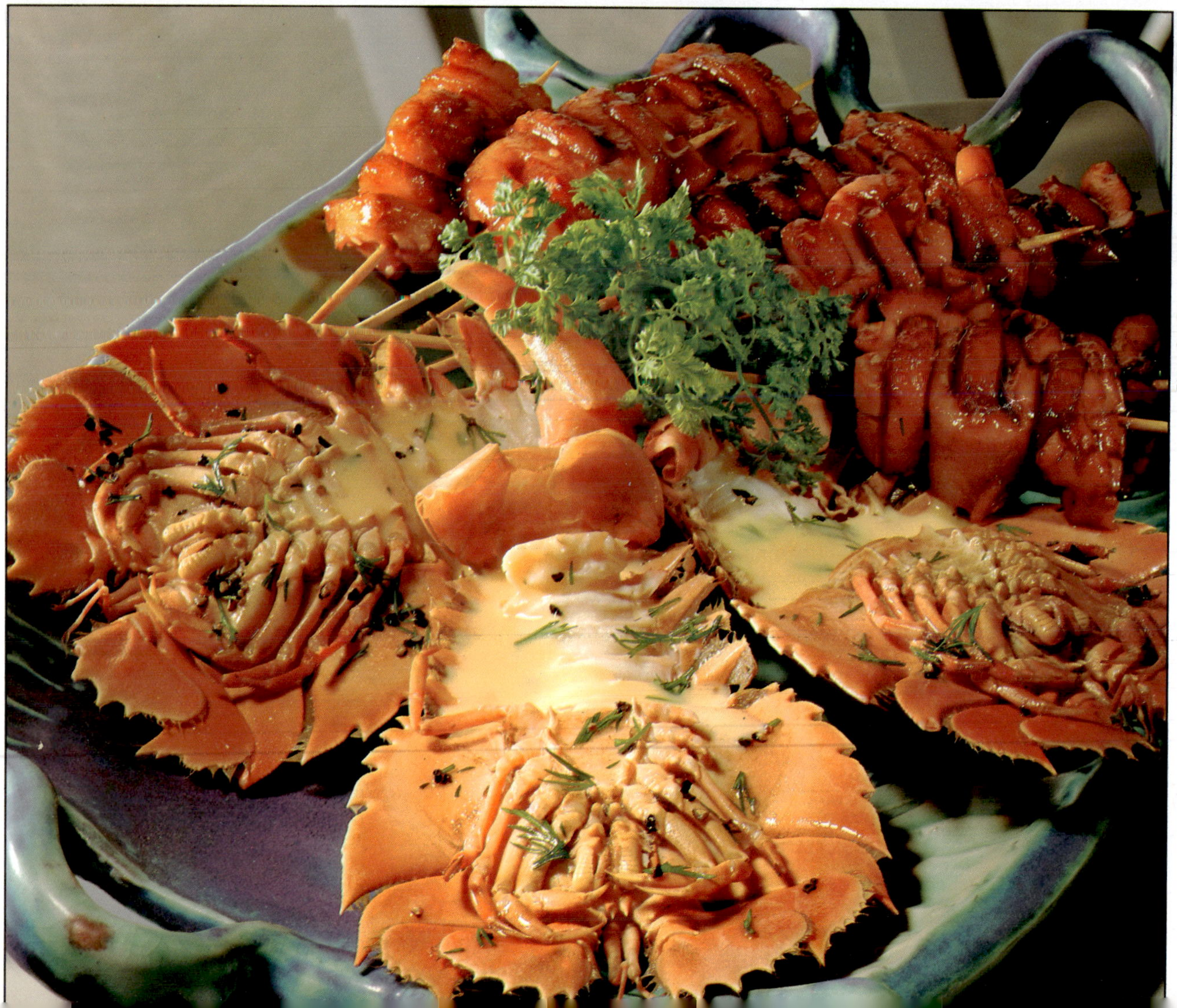

Plate: Clay Things; table, Outdoor Leisure & Building Centre

BUTTERFLIED SARDINES WITH MINTED PINEAPPLE SAUCE

Sardines can be prepared for cooking several hours ahead; keep, covered, in refrigerator. Toss in flour just before cooking. Sauce, without mint, can be prepared up to a day ahead; keep, covered, in refrigerator. Serve sardines as soon as they are cooked. This recipe is not suitable to freeze.

750g sardines
plain flour
MINTED PINEAPPLE SAUCE
225g can unsweetened pineapple pieces
15g butter
1 small onion, finely chopped
2 teaspoons cornflour
½ cup water
1 tablespoon chopped fresh mint

Remove heads and backbones from sardines. Toss sardines in flour, cook on well-greased hot plate or in frying pan, turning occasionally, until sardines are browned and tender. Serve with sauce.

Minted Pineapple Sauce: Blend or process undrained pineapple until finely chopped. Heat butter in saucepan, add onion, stir over heat for about 2 minutes (or microwave on HIGH for 3 minutes) or until onion is soft. Blend cornflour with a little of the water, add the remaining water to pan with pineapple, stir constantly over high heat (or microwave on HIGH for about 3 minutes) until sauce boils and thickens. Stir in mint.

Serves 4.

SALMON WITH SOUR CREAM STUFFED POTATOES

We used canned salmon in this recipe, but fresh Atlantic salmon or ocean trout can be used. Poach 200g of the fish in simmering water for a few minutes or until tender, drain well, flake with fork. Potatoes can be prepared ready for final cooking up to 2 hours ahead, cook just before serving. This recipe is not suitable to freeze or microwave.

6 medium potatoes
60g butter, melted
salt
210g can salmon, drained
¼ cup sour cream
2 green shallots, chopped
1 tablespoon chopped fresh dill
1 tablespoon grated parmesan cheese
1 tablespoon lemon juice

Brush each potato with butter, sprinkle with salt, wrap each potato securely in foil. Cook in ashes of barbecue or bake in moderate oven for about 50 minutes or until potatoes are tender. Cool potatoes for 5 minutes, cut top from each potato, carefully scoop out pulp and mash with fork until smooth. You will need only 1½ cups mashed potato for this recipe.

Combine reserved mashed potato, salmon, sour cream, shallots, dill, cheese and lemon juice in bowl. Spoon into potatoes, wrap potatoes individually in foil. Barbecue or bake until heated through.

Makes 6.

FISH PARCELS WITH LEMON SAUCE

We used bream fillets for this recipe. Sauce can be made several hours ahead; keep, covered, in refrigerator. Reheat just before serving. Recipe unsuitable to freeze or microwave.

1 medium red pepper, sliced
1 medium green pepper, sliced
100g baby mushrooms, sliced
1 tablespoon chopped fresh parsley
4 white fish fillets
LEMON SAUCE
1 small chicken stock cube, crumbled
¾ cup water
2 tablespoons lemon juice
2 tablespoons chopped fresh parsley
2 teaspoons cornflour
1 tablespoon water, extra

Combine peppers, mushrooms and parsley in bowl. Place each fillet onto a large piece of foil, top with vegetable mixture, seal to make a parcel. Barbecue over high heat for about 8 minutes or until fish are cooked through. Serve with lemon sauce.

Lemon Sauce: Combine stock cube, water, lemon juice and parsley in small saucepan, bring to boil. Stir in cornflour blended with extra water, stir constantly over high heat until sauce boils and thickens.

Serves 4.

ABOVE: From left: Salmon with Sour Cream Stuffed Potatoes; Fish Parcels with Lemon Sauce. LEFT: From top; Marinated Squid and Water Chestnut Kebabs; Balmain Bugs with Lime Butter. ABOVE LEFT: Butterflied Sardines with Minted Pineapple Sauce.

LOBSTER TAILS WITH ORANGE PINE NUT BUTTER

Butter can be prepared up to a week ahead; keep in plastic wrap in refrigerator or freeze for up to 2 months. Cook lobster just before serving. This recipe is not suitable to microwave.

6 small uncooked lobster tails
ORANGE PINE NUT BUTTER
185g butter
1 teaspoon grated orange rind
2 tablespoons orange juice
1 tablespoon chopped fresh parsley
1 tablespoon chopped fresh dill
1 tablespoon chopped fresh chives
2 tablespoons pine nuts, toasted

Cut away skin underneath tails to expose lobster flesh. Barbecue or grill until tender. Top with sliced orange pine nut butter just before serving.

Orange Pine Nut Butter: Process butter, rind, juice, herbs and pine nuts until smooth. Spoon mixture onto greaseproof paper or foil in a log shape, roll up firmly, refrigerate 1 hour or until firm.

Serves 6.

SQUID WITH CHUTNEY, HONEY AND GARLIC

Squid can be prepared a day ahead; keep, covered, in refrigerator. This recipe is not suitable to freeze or microwave.

1kg baby squid hoods
1 tablespoon sweet fruit chutney
¼ cup lemon juice
2 tablespoons French dressing
2 cloves garlic, crushed
1 tablespoon honey
1 tablespoon chopped fresh coriander

Make cuts about ½cm apart in 1 side of each squid hood. Place squid in large bowl with chutney, juice, dressing, garlic and honey. Mix well, cover, stand for 2 hours or overnight. Barbecue or grill for about 2 minutes or until squid are tender; turn often during cooking. Sprinkle with coriander before serving.

Serves 4.

BELOW: Lobster Tails with Orange Pine Nut Butter. RIGHT: From top: Squid with Chutney, Honey and Garlic; Octopus with Pine Nuts, Sultanas and Basil.

OCTOPUS WITH PINE NUTS, SULTANAS AND BASIL

Octopus can be prepared a day ahead; keep, covered, in refrigerator. This recipe is not suitable to freeze or microwave.

1kg baby octopus
½ cup pine nuts
¼ cup sultanas
½ teaspoon grated lemon rind
½ cup lemon juice
2 cloves garlic, crushed
½ cup fresh basil leaves
⅓ cup olive oil
1 teaspoon cracked black peppercorns

Remove and discard heads from octopus, place octopus in large bowl. Blend or process pine nuts, sultanas, rind, juice, garlic, basil, oil and peppercorns until almost smooth (mixture should be combined but remain a little coarse). Pour pine nut mixture over octopus, mix well, cover, refrigerate for about 2 hours or overnight. Barbecue octopus for about 1 minute on each side or until tender.

Serves 4.

SNAPPER WITH SHALLOTS AND RED PEPPER SEASONING

We used a whole snapper in this recipe. The fish can be prepared for cooking a day ahead; keep, covered, in refrigerator. This recipe is not suitable to freeze or microwave.

**30g butter
6 green shallots, chopped
1 small red pepper, finely chopped
2 cloves garlic, crushed
1 cup stale breadcrumbs
1 medium snapper
¼ cup lemon juice**

Melt butter in small saucepan, add shallots, pepper and garlic. Stir over medium heat for about 3 minutes or until pepper is soft. Remove from heat, stir in breadcrumbs. Press mixture into cavity of fish, cook over medium heat on well-greased barbecue hot plate or in frying pan for about 20 minutes or until fish is tender. Pour juice over fish just before serving.
　Serves 2.

RIGHT: From top: Barbecued Fish with Herb and Bacon Butter; Skewered Honeyed Prawns. BELOW: Snapper with Shallots and Red Pepper Seasoning. BELOW RIGHT: Carpet Bag Steak Sizzlers. ABOVE RIGHT: Olive Seasoned Fish Cutlets.

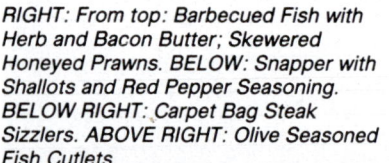

BARBECUED FISH WITH HERB AND BACON BUTTER

We used flathead for this recipe. Fish can be prepared up to a day ahead; cook just before serving. This recipe is not suitable to freeze or microwave.

**250g butter
4 bacon rashers, chopped
¼ cup chopped fresh parsley
1 tablespoon chopped fresh chives
1 tablespoon chopped fresh thyme
¼ cup grated parmesan cheese
1 clove garlic, crushed
1 small onion, chopped
1 tablespoon lemon juice
6 small whole white fish**

Beat butter in small bowl until creamy, stir in bacon, herbs, cheese, garlic, onion and lemon juice. Cut back fins from fish, trim remaining fins. Using sharp knife, cut down each side of backbone to form two pockets; do not cut right through. Spread butter mixture into each pocket, wrap each fish in foil, barbecue (or bake fish for about 30 minutes in moderate oven) or until fish are tender.
　Serves 6.

SKEWERED HONEYED PRAWNS

Prawns can be prepared up to a day ahead; cook just before serving. This recipe is not suitable to freeze or microwave.

1kg uncooked king prawns
2 tablespoons light soy sauce
3 teaspoons hoisin sauce
1 tablespoon barbecue sauce
1 teaspoon chilli sauce
1 tablespoon honey
1 tablespoon oil
1 tablespoon dry sherry
2 cloves garlic, crushed

Shell prawns, leaving tails intact. Combine sauces, honey, oil, sherry and garlic in large bowl, add prawns, mix well. Cover, refrigerate for 2 hours. Thread prawns onto skewers, barbecue or grill over high heat until prawns are tender. Brush with marinade during cooking.

Serves 4.

OLIVE SEASONED FISH CUTLETS

We used snapper cutlets (with bone in) for this recipe. Cutlets can be seasoned up to a day ahead; keep, covered, in refrigerator. This recipe is not suitable to freeze or microwave.

4 white fish cutlets
⅓ cup stuffed olives, chopped
¼ cup seeded mustard
2 tablespoons sweet fruit chutney
2 tablespoons chopped fresh parsley
2 teaspoons chopped fresh coriander
1 tablespoon chopped fresh basil
2 tablespoons chopped fresh chives
2 cups (250g) stale breadcrumbs
90g butter

Remove bones from cutlets by cutting through 1 end of cutlets. Combine olives, mustard, chutney, herbs and breadcrumbs in large bowl. Divide olive mixture between cutlets, secure open ends with toothpicks. Heat butter on hot plate or in large frying pan. Add cutlets, cook over high heat for about 5 minutes on each side or until they are cooked through.

Serves 4.

CARPET BAG STEAK SIZZLERS

Steaks can be filled with oysters several hours ahead; keep, covered, in refrigerator. This recipe is not suitable to freeze or microwave.

16 oysters
1 tablespoon lemon juice
4 thick beef eye-fillet steaks
30g butter, melted
SPICY SAUCE
¼ cup Father's Favourite sauce
2 tablespoons water
1 tablespoon chopped fresh mint

Combine oysters and lemon juice in small bowl, stand for at least 15 minutes. Cut a small pocket in the side of each steak. Fill pockets with oysters, secure openings with toothpicks. Cook steaks on greased hot plate or in frying pan, turning frequently until cooked as desired. Brush steaks with butter during cooking. Serve steaks with sauce.

Spicy Sauce: Combine all ingredients in jug. Serve a little over hot steaks.

Serves 4.

Plates: Clay Things

JUST FOR KIDS

110

Take the youngsters on a voyage of flavour discoveries with our recipes and give them a life-long taste for seafood the healthy way. We enjoyed devising dishes they can't wait to devour, so here you will find crunchy finger foods and novelties for anytime (they are great for parties, too). As well, there are some very tempting but simple meals. All recipes are quick, and some easy enough for kids to prepare.

CRACKLY FISH STRIPS

We used gemfish fillets in this recipe. Strips can be prepared for cooking up to a day ahead; keep, covered, in refrigerator or freeze for up to 2 months. This recipe is not suitable to freeze or microwave.

300g white fish fillets
plain flour
1 egg, lightly beaten
1 tablespoon milk
2½ cups Rice Bubbles
oil for deep-frying

Cut fish into 1cm strips, toss in flour, shake off excess flour. Dip fish into combined egg and milk, then roll in lightly crushed Rice Bubbles. Deep-fry fish, several pieces at a time, in hot oil until strips are golden brown; drain on absorbent paper.
Serves 4.

FISH SANDWICHES

Sandwiches can be prepared several hours before they are required; keep, covered, in refrigerator. This recipe is not suitable to freeze.

16 slices wholemeal bread
210g can salmon, drained
250g packet cream cheese
tiny pinch saffron powder
1 tablespoon tomato paste
2 gherkins, sliced
4 pitted black olives, sliced
2 small tomatoes, sliced
75g baby mushrooms, sliced
½ x 150g punnet alfalfa sprouts

Lightly toast bread, cut into fish shapes, as pictured. Blend or process salmon, cheese, saffron and tomato paste until smooth; spread evenly over fish shapes. Place half the fish onto plates, add gherkins and olives (reserving 8 slices of each for eyes) and tomatoes. Top with remaining fish. Decorate with mushrooms, reserved gherkins, olives, sprouts.
Makes 8.

FISH AND VEGETABLE PASTIES

We used ocean perch and packaged frozen vegetables in this recipe (cook vegetables as directed on packet). Left-over cooked vegetables of your choice can be used; chop all vegetables into 1cm cubes. Pasties can be prepared several hours before cooking; keep, covered, in refrigerator. This recipe is not suitable to freeze or microwave.

½ cup water
¼ cup lemon juice
¼ cup white vinegar
4 green shallots, chopped
300g white fish fillets, chopped
2 egg yolks
2 tablespoons sour cream
1 small chicken stock cube, crumbled
1 cup grated tasty cheese
1 tablespoon chopped fresh parsley
1 cup cooked mixed vegetables
2 sheets ready-rolled puff pastry
1 egg, lightly beaten
1 tablespoon sesame seeds

Combine water, lemon juice, vinegar and shallots in medium frying pan, cover, bring to boil. Reduce heat, add fish, simmer for 5 minutes. Strain fish from stock, discard stock. Combine egg yolks, sour cream, stock cube, cheese and parsley in medium bowl, stir in fish and vegetables. Divide mixture into 4 portions.
 Cut 2 12cm circles from each sheet of pastry. Divide filling between pastry circles, fold in half, pinch edges together with fingers. Place each pastie upright on greased oven tray, brush with egg, sprinkle with sesame seeds, bake in moderately hot oven for about 20 minutes or until golden brown. Stand for 10 minutes before serving.
Makes 4.

From left: Crackly Fish Strips; Fish Sandwiches.

TASTY FISH SAUSAGES

We used bream fillets for this recipe. Sausages are best prepared just before serving. This recipe is not suitable to freeze or microwave.

**500g white fish fillets
2 green shallots, finely chopped
2 tablespoons chopped fresh parsley
1 small carrot, grated
1 tablespoon lemon juice
¼ cup stale breadcrumbs
2 eggs, lightly beaten
plain flour
2 tablespoons oil
15g butter**

Blend, process or mince fish until fine. Combine shallots, parsley, carrot, juice, breadcrumbs and eggs in large bowl. Stir in fish. Divide mixture into 12, shape into sausages, toss lightly in flour. Heat oil and butter in large frying pan, add sausages, cook over medium heat for about 10 minutes or until the sausages are browned and cooked through.

Makes 12.

STIR-FRIED FISH AND MUSHROOMS IN LETTUCE CUPS

We used mullet fillets in this dish. Stir-fry is best served immediately it is prepared. This recipe is not suitable to freeze or microwave.

**500g oily fish fillets
¼ cup oil
1 clove garlic, crushed
2 teaspoons grated fresh ginger
230g can water chestnuts, drained, sliced
250g baby mushrooms, sliced
1 tablespoon cornflour
⅔ cup water
1½ tablespoons light soy sauce
½ teaspoon castor sugar
1 small chicken stock cube, crumbled
1 small red Spanish onion, sliced
1 small lettuce**

Process or mince fish until fine. Heat oil in wok or large frying pan, add garlic and ginger, stir-fry for 1 minute. Add chestnuts and mushrooms, stir-fry until mushrooms are just tender. Add fish, stir-fry for 1 minute.

Blend cornflour with water, stir into fish mixture with sauce, sugar and stock cube, stir-fry constantly until mixture boils and thickens. Serve topped with onion in lettuce cups.

Serves 4.

LEFT: From top: Fish and Vegetable Pasties; Tasty Fish Sausages. ABOVE: Stir-Fried Fish and Mushrooms in Lettuce Cups.

FISH ROLLS WITH SWEET AND SOUR SAUCE

We used thick, ocean perch fillets for this recipe. Sauce can be made up to several days ahead; keep, covered, in refrigerator. Recipe unsuitable to freeze. Rolls unsuitable to microwave.

500g white fish fillets
2 tablespoons mayonnaise
⅔ cup stale white breadcrumbs
⅔ cup grated carrot
2 green shallots, chopped
1 stick celery, chopped
2 sheets ready-rolled puff pastry
1 egg, lightly beaten
SWEET AND SOUR SAUCE
1 tablespoon cornflour
1 cup sweetened pineapple juice
½ cup white vinegar
2 tablespoons sugar
2 tablespoons tomato sauce

Blend or process fish, mayonnaise and breadcrumbs until smooth. Transfer mixture to large bowl, add the carrot, shallots and celery, stir to combine.

Cut each pastry sheet into 3 even strips. Place fish mixture into a piping bag without a tube. Pipe fish mixture along 1 edge of each pastry strip. Brush opposite edge with egg, fold pastry over to enclose filling completely. Brush rolls with egg, cut each roll into 6 pieces.

Place rolls onto lightly greased oven trays, bake in moderately hot oven for 20 minutes or until golden brown. Serve rolls hot or cold with hot or cold sauce for dipping.

Sweet and Sour Sauce: Blend cornflour with a little of the pineapple juice in small saucepan, stir in remaining pineapple juice, vinegar, sugar and tomato sauce. Stir constantly over heat until sauce boils and thickens (or microwave on HIGH for about 3 minutes).

Makes 36.

TUNA AND KUMARA FRITTATA

Frittata is best served immediately it is made. This recipe is not suitable to freeze or microwave.

250g kumara
185g can chunk-style tuna, drained
60g butter
1 small onion, finely chopped
1 large tomato, finely chopped
2 tablespoons chopped fresh parsley
2 eggs, lightly beaten
2 teaspoons grated orange rind
½ cup grated processed cheddar cheese

Boil, steam or microwave unpeeled kumara until tender; drain. Place in cold water for about 10 minutes or until cool; drain. Press excess moisture from tuna, flake with fork.

Melt half the butter in small frying pan, add onion, stir constantly over medium heat for about 2 minutes or until onion is soft. Add tomato, cook for about 5 minutes or until mixture is thickened slightly. Place tomato mixture in large bowl; cool. Peel kumara, cut into chunks, add to tomato mixture with tuna, parsley, eggs, rind and cheese; stir gently until combined.

Heat remaining butter in small frying pan, add tuna mixture, cook over medium heat for about 3 minutes or until base is cooked and lightly browned. Place pan under hot griller for about 2 minutes or until golden brown and set. Serve cut in wedges.

Serves 2 to 4

SARDINE FINGER SANDWICHES

We used a light wholemeal bread for this recipe. Sandwiches are best prepared just before serving. This recipe is not suitable to freeze or microwave.

6 slices bread
110g can sardines, drained
2 tablespoons mayonnaise
1 green shallot, sliced
½ teaspoon curry powder
2 eggs, lightly beaten
2 tablespoons milk
60g butter

Trim crusts from bread. Combine mashed sardines, mayonnaise, shallot and curry powder in small bowl. Spread sardine mixture onto 3 slices of the bread, top with remaining bread, press top slices on firmly. Cut each sandwich into 3 pieces, dip into combined eggs and milk. Melt butter in large frying pan, add sandwiches, cook on both sides until golden brown.

Makes 9.

LEFT: From top: Tuna and Kumara Frittata; Fish Rolls with Sweet and Sour Sauce.

SAUCY FISH BALLS WITH SPAGHETTI

We used ling fillets for this recipe. Sauce is best prepared just before serving. This recipe is not suitable to freeze.

4 spinach (silver beet) leaves
500g white fish fillets
2 tablespoons chopped fresh chives
1 egg, lightly beaten
1 teaspoon oil
1 small onion, chopped
2 cloves garlic, crushed
1 small red pepper, finely chopped
2 x 410g cans tomatoes
1 tablespoon tomato paste
2 teaspoons chopped fresh basil
1 teaspoon sugar
250g spaghetti
2 tablespoons grated fresh parmesan cheese

Boil, steam or microwave spinach until tender; drain, chop. Blend or process fish until smooth, transfer to medium bowl, stir in spinach, chives and egg, shape into 16 balls.

Heat oil in large saucepan, add onion and garlic, stir constantly over medium heat for about 2 minutes (or microwave on HIGH for about 3 minutes) or until onion is soft.

Add pepper, undrained crushed tomatoes, paste, basil and sugar, bring to boil. Reduce heat, simmer, uncovered, for about 25 minutes (or microwave on HIGH for about 20 minutes) or until sauce is thickened. Add fish balls, cook further 15 minutes (or microwave on HIGH for about 7 minutes) until fish is cooked.

Gradually add spaghetti to large saucepan of boiling water, boil, uncovered, for about 12 minutes or until spaghetti is just tender; drain. Serve sauce over hot spaghetti. Serve topped with cheese.

Serves 4.

TUNA CREPE STACK

Filled crêpes can be prepared up to a day ahead; keep, covered, in refrigerator. Unfilled crepes can be frozen for up to 2 months, layered with freezer or plastic wrap. Sauce unsuitable to freeze.

CREPES
¾ cup plain flour
3 eggs, lightly beaten
1 tablespoon oil
1 cup milk
½ cup grated tasty cheese
TUNA SAUCE
60g butter
1 medium onion, chopped
2 tablespoons plain flour
1½ cups milk
425g can tuna in brine, drained
½ cup frozen peas, thawed
1 tablespoon chopped fresh parsley
1 cup grated tasty cheese

Crêpes: Sift flour into medium bowl, make well in centre, add eggs, oil and ¼ cup of the milk; beat until smooth. Beat in remaining milk. Pour batter into jug, refrigerate for 30 minutes.

Heat heavy-based crêpe pan, grease lightly. Pour 2 to 3 tablespoons batter into pan, swirling batter evenly around pan to coat base. Cook over medium heat until crêpe is lightly browned; turn crêpe, lightly brown other side; turn onto plate. Use remaining batter to make about 12 crêpes.

Place a crêpe onto plate, spread with ¼ cup of tuna sauce, continue layering with remaining crêpes and sauce. Sprinkle top with cheese, bake in moderate oven for about 10 minutes (or microwave on HIGH for about 3 minutes) or until cheese is melted.

Tuna Sauce: Heat butter in medium saucepan, add onion, stir constantly over medium heat (or microwave on HIGH for about 3 minutes) or until onion is soft. Stir in flour, cook, stirring, for 2 minutes. Gradually stir in milk, stir constantly over high heat until mixture boils and thickens (or microwave on HIGH for about 3 minutes, stirring occasionally). Add flaked tuna, peas, parsley and cheese; stir until mixture is combined.

Serves 6.

Table: The Itchy Palm

LEFT: From top: Sardine Finger Sandwiches; Saucy Fish Balls with Spaghetti. RIGHT: Clockwise from top left: Mini Anchovy Pizzas; Tuna Crêpe Stack; Torpedoes with Creamy Tomato Sauce.

MINI ANCHOVY PIZZAS

Uncooked pizzas can be frozen for 2 months; cook while frozen for about 25 minutes. This recipe is not suitable to microwave.

15g compressed yeast
½ teaspoon sugar
½ cup warm water
1½ cups plain flour
2 tablespoons oil
⅓ cup tomato paste
100g baby mushrooms, sliced
45g can anchovy fillets, drained, sliced
1 small red pepper, sliced
¼ cup pitted black olives, chopped
1 cup grated mozzarella cheese
¼ cup grated parmesan cheese

Combine yeast and sugar with water in bowl, cover, stand in warm place for about 10 minutes or until mixture is foamy. Sift flour into large bowl, make well in centre, stir in yeast mixture, then oil. Turn onto lightly floured surface, knead lightly for about 10 minutes or until the dough is smooth and elastic.

Return dough to lightly oiled bowl, cover, stand in warm place for about 30 minutes or until dough has doubled in bulk. Knead dough into smooth ball, divide dough into 6 pieces, roll into 14cm rounds. Place onto lightly greased oven trays.

Spread each round with tomato paste, sprinkle with mushrooms, anchovies, pepper, olives and combined cheeses. Bake in moderately hot oven for about 15 minutes or until golden brown.

Makes 6.

TORPEDOES WITH CREAMY TOMATO SAUCE

We used redfish fillets in this recipe. Torpedoes can be crumbed up to a day ahead; keep, covered, in refrigerator. This recipe is not suitable to freeze. Prepared torpedoes are not suitable to microwave.

250g white fish fillets
2 medium potatoes, chopped
60g butter
1 medium onion, chopped
1 tablespoon chopped fresh parsley
1 teaspoon grated lemon rind
1 tablespoon tomato sauce
plain flour
1 egg, lightly beaten
¼ cup milk
2 cups stale white breadcrumbs
oil for deep-frying
CREAMY TOMATO SAUCE
¼ cup sour cream
¼ cup tomato sauce

Plates: Villa Italiana

Blend or process fish until smooth. Boil, steam or microwave potatoes until tender.

Heat butter in small frying pan, add onion, stir constantly over medium heat for about 2 minutes (or microwave on HIGH for about 3 minutes) or until onion is soft. Stir in parsley, rind and sauce; cool.

Mash potatoes in large bowl, stir in fish and onion mixture, cover, refrigerate for about 1 hour or until firm.

Divide fish mixture into 8, shape into 11cm lengths, insert wooden skewer through each length. Coat lightly in flour, shake off excess flour. Dip into combined egg and milk, toss in breadcrumbs. Deep-fry torpedoes in hot oil until golden brown and crisp. Drain on absorbent paper, serve hot with sauce.

Creamy Tomato Sauce: Combine cream and sauce in small bowl.

Makes 8.

THE FACTS

All varieties of seafood share a rich nutritional bounty with plenty of protein, minerals and vitamins. As a bonus, they are low in fat and kilojoules.

Iron, zinc and iodine are found in abundance in seafood, especially in molluscs. The vitamins present include the full range of B group vitamins and vitamin E. Some fish also supply vitamins A and D.

To add to their virtues, the small amount of fat in fish contains essential omega 3 fatty acids which can help reduce the risk of heart disease and, possibly, a number of other health problems.

Years ago, it was thought that some seafood had a high level of cholesterol. In fact, only prawns have significant quantities, and even this is of little importance since they contain very little saturated fat. Most of the cholesterol in the blood is made in the body from saturated fats in foods, rather than coming from cholesterol already present in foods.

Nutritionists love to recommend foods which taste as good as they are healthy. Seafood absolutely fills the bill.
— ROSEMARY STANTON

BUYING, FREEZING AND STORING TIPS

WHOLE FISH
To buy: choose fish with clear bulging eyes and very black pupils; firm, lustrous skin with tight scales; bright red gills and a pleasant sea smell.
To freeze: gill and gut fish, wrap carefully in foil, avoid piercing foil. Place into freezer bag, remove air, seal, date and label. Freeze white fish up to 6 months, 3 months for oily fish.
To store: remove scales, wash cavity well, scrape any blood from backbone. Gently shake off excess water, place into airtight container, or onto a plate, cover with plastic wrap. Refrigerate for up to 3 days.

FISH FILLETS AND CUTLETS
To buy: flesh should have a slightly shiny surface, be firm (not spongy) and have a pleasant sea smell.
To freeze: quickly and gently rinse under cold water, shake off excess water, wrap individually in freezer wrap, stack in appropriate serving portions. Place into freezer bag, remove air, seal, date and label. Freeze white fish for up to 6 months; 3 months for oily fish.
To store: quickly and gently rinse fish under cold water, gently shake off excess water, place fish into an airtight container or onto a plate, cover with plastic wrap. Refrigerate for up to 3 days.

SMOKED FISH
To buy: flesh should be firm with a pleasant smell, avoid sticky surface.
To freeze: as for fresh fish, but saltiness can increase during freezing and smoked flavour decrease slightly. Freeze for up to 3 months.
To store: place in airtight container or wrap in foil. Refrigerate up to 5 days.

CRUSTACEANS
(crabs, lobsters/crayfish, Balmain bugs, yabbies, marron and scampi)
To buy: these are available cooked, uncooked and live.
When cooked, they are orange in colour with no black discolouration, particularly at the joints. Shells should be firmly intact (lobster tails should be curled) and have a pleasant sea smell.
When uncooked, they are known as "green" though they may sometimes be another colour, such as the blue swimmer crab. Shells should be firm and have a pleasant sea smell.
When live, look for active animals for freshest flavour. These must be killed as humanely as possible. We recommend drowning in fresh water or freezing for 6 to 8 hours before cooking. Use as directed in recipes. We do not recommend cooking live animals as it is unnecessarily cruel and will toughen the meat.
To freeze: cooked and uncooked, they should be cleaned well then wrapped unshelled in foil; avoid piercing foil. Place into freezer bag, remove air, seal, date and label. Freeze for up to 3 months.
To store: cooked and uncooked, rinse quickly under cold water, shake off excess water, place unshelled into airtight container or onto a plate, cover with plastic wrap. Refrigerate up to 3 days.

CRUSTACEANS
(prawns)
To buy: these are cooked and uncooked (known as green). when cooked, they are orange in colour. Shells should be firmly intact and have a pleasant sea smell.
When uncooked, they should be firm and have a pleasant sea smell.
To freeze: cooked and uncooked, they are best frozen unshelled. Place into container, barely cover with tap water, allowing space for water to expand during freezing, seal and freeze like an ice block for up to 3 months. To defrost, place under cold running water to melt the ice then refrigerate prawns for several hours or until they reach an edible temperature.
To store: cooked and uncooked, follow instructions as for crab and lobster.

MOLLUSCS
(for example, mussels, pipis, oysters, clams, cockles etc)
To buy: molluscs should have a pleasant sea smell and be firmly closed (except for the green-lipped New Zealand mussels).
To freeze: not recommended.

To store: place molluscs into colander, cover with a damp cloth, then place colander in a slightly larger bowl; place in the lowest section of the refrigerator, use within 3 days.
To cook: wash and scrub shells (remove fibrous beards from mussels by pulling firmly). Check cooking suitability on Your Guide to Seafood chart. As shells open, remove from heat. Shells that do not open when most have opened can be prised open with a blunt knife. If the meat is firm and intact and smells good, include with the rest. It was previously thought that all unopened molluscs should be discarded but it is now known that some shells do not open because the meat is attached on both sides.

MOLLUSCS
(for example, squid (calamari), octopus and cuttlefish)
To buy: choose those with a mottled brown skin, avoid any with a dark purple-black colouring.
To freeze: gut, clean and wash well. Wrap in freezer wrap, place in freezer bag, remove air, seal, date and label. Freeze for up to 3 months.
To store: rinse quickly under cold water, shake off excess water, place into an airtight container or onto a plate, cover with plastic wrap. Refrigerate for up to 3 days. These can be cleaned and prepared before storing, if preferred; keep, covered, in refrigerator for up to 3 days.
To cook: these go through a cooking process of tender to tough then back to tender. All require very quick cooking (for example, 1 minute for squid and cuttlefish and 3 to 4 minutes for octopus) to be tender. Alternatively, depending on individual recipes, if the heat is lowered to simmer and cooking time extended to about 45 minutes the flesh will tenderise again.

TIPS ON COOKING SEAFOOD IN A MICROWAVE OVEN
- Careful timing and checking when microwaving seafood is important to prevent over-cooking. Fish is cooked when opaque or white in colour. Cover during cooking.
- Fold thin tail ends under fillets to give uniform thickness in oven.
- Arrange fish and shellfish with the thickest parts towards the outer edge of the dish.
- Avoid stacking seafood, a single layer of food will ensure more even and faster cooking.
- When microwaving fish, 70 per cent power is usually enough. Whole fish can be given up to 3 minutes on 100 per cent power, then reduced to 70 per cent for the rest of the cooking time. Shellfish and molluscs which are protected by a shell can be microwaved on 100 per cent power.
- Pierce eyes of whole fish and cover the thinner tail ends with lightly greased foil for half the cooking time to prevent over-cooking.
- Use a knife to cut slashes in thick parts of whole fish or fish fillets to allow for more even cooking.
- Always allow up to 2 minutes standing time for fish after microwaving to complete cooking.

OVEN TEMPERATURES

Electric Temperatures	Celsius	Fahrenheit	Gas Temperatures	Celsius	Fahrenheit
Very slow	120	250	Very slow	120	250
Slow	150	300	Slow	150	300
Moderately slow	160-180	325-350	Moderately slow	160	325
Moderate	180-200	375-400	Moderate	180	350
Moderately hot	210-230	425-450	Moderately hot	190	375
Hot	240-250	475-500	Hot	200	400
Very hot	260	525-550	Very hot	230	450

CUP AND SPOON MEASURES
Recipes in this book use this standard metric equipment approved by the Australian Standards Association:
(a) 250 millilitre cup for measuring liquids. A litre jug (capacity 4 cups) is also available.
(b) a graduated set of cups — measuring 1 cup, half, third and quarter cup — for items such as flour, sugar, etc. When measuring in these fractional cups, level off at the brim.
(c) a graduated set of four spoons: tablespoon (20 millilitre liquid capacity), teaspoon (5 millilitre), half and quarter teaspoons. The Australian, British and American teaspoon each has 5ml capacity.

All spoon measurements are level.
Note: We have used large eggs with an average weight of 61g each in all recipes.

APPROXIMATE CUP AND SPOON CONVERSION CHART

Australian	American & British
1 cup	1¼ cups
¾ cup	1 cup
⅔ cup	¾ cup
½ cup	⅔ cup
⅓ cup	½ cup
¼ cup	⅓ cup
2 tablespoons	¼ cup
1 tablespoon	3 teaspoons

SEAFOOD PREPARATION
...our expert shows how

CLEAN FISH
Cut fish open, as shown; remove and discard entrails.

SCALE FISH
Hold fish firmly by the tail. Use blunt knife to remove scales, working from tail to head.

FILLETING A ROUND FISH
(such as bream, snapper and blackfish) Cut through half of fish along front fin.

Starting at head of fish, cut flat against spine; move knife along spine towards tail with a "press and gentle push" motion.

Picture shows rib cage and fillet cut away. Turn fish over, repeat on other side.

SKINNING FILLETS
Cut a little of the flesh from the skin at tail end. Hold the skin with salted fingers at tail end and continue cutting away flesh, keeping knife flat against the skin.

FILLETING FLAT FISH
Cut through centre of fish along spine from head towards tail.

Carefully cut flesh away from fish, scraping blade of knife along bones as you cut.

SKINNING A WHOLE FLAT FISH
Nick skin at tail end of fish, use salt on fingers to give grip. Hold fish firmly by the tail, pull skin in opposite direction.

BONING WHOLE FISH
Remove head. Cut through flesh from gills to tail along belly. Cut through flesh on either side of backbone so fish can be spread out flat, avoid cutting into the skin.

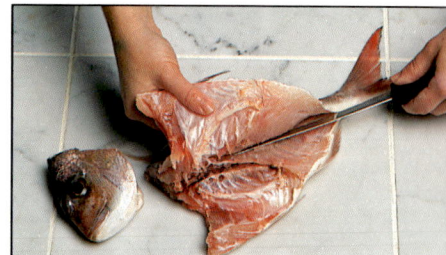

Spread fish out flat, cut out backbone using scissors or knife.

Spread fish out flat, trim off rib bones on each side.

HOW TO BUTTERFLY GARFISH AND SARDINES
Cut off heads and remove entrails.

Cut through under-side to backbone; rinse under cold water. Cut backbone through at tail end without piercing skin. Pull backbone out towards head end to remove. Remove small bones.

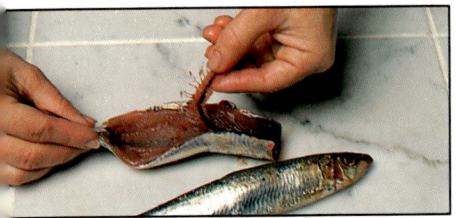

Butterflied fish with bones removed.

SHELLING PRAWNS
Hold head firmly and twist to remove from body of prawn.

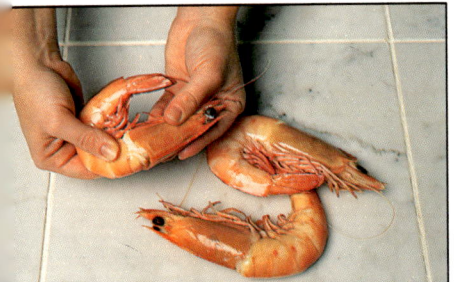

Remove shell and legs from body without removing tail shell.

Remove two tail fins.

Slip tail shell from prawn.

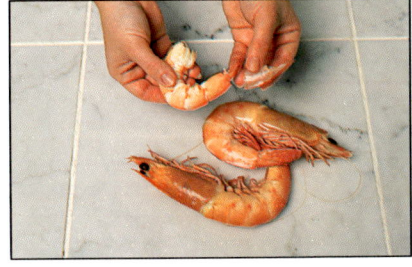

Remove back vein from prawn.

PREPARING A COOKED LOBSTER (CRAYFISH)
Place lobster with back down, cut through chest and tail.

Turn lobster around and cut through head.

Pull lobster halves apart. Discard white gills and grey thread running down centre back of tail. The liver or creamy green area can be used to make sauce. Use fingers to remove meat from tail sections.

PREPARING COOKED BALMAIN BUGS
Place back down. Cut tail from body.

Cut through tail lengthways.

Remove back vein from tail.

Remove meat from tail halves.

SHUCKING OYSTERS
Insert strong short-bladed rigid knife (oyster knife) next to hinge between the 2 shells. Twist knife to pop top shell open.

• Remove top shell, loosen oyster with knife. Turn oyster over and return to washed and dried shell for serving.

PREPARING MUSSELS FOR COOKING
(1kg mussels in shells yields 250g meat)
To clean mussels, pull away the seaweed thread or "beard". Use a stiff brush to scrub under cold water. Boil, steam or microwave to open.

PREPARING CUTTLEFISH
Gently cut through to centre of cuttlefish on soft side, to avoid breaking the black ink sac. The ink sac is edible; however, it can be a little messy. Rinse away under cold running water.
Gently pull head and tentacles from body.

Remove cuttle bone from body. Firmly pull skin away from meat, wash well.

Cut into slices or cut diamond pattern into cuttlefish pieces without cutting right through (known as honeycombing).

PREPARING OCTOPUS
Cut head from tentacles just below eyes.

Cut eyes away from head, discard eyes. Remove body "beak" from centre of legs by pushing finger through centre and beak should pop out; discard beak.

Pull skin gently away from head; wash head and tentacles thoroughly.

PREPARING SQUID
Gently pull head and entrails away from body of squid. Remove clear backbone (quill) from inside body.

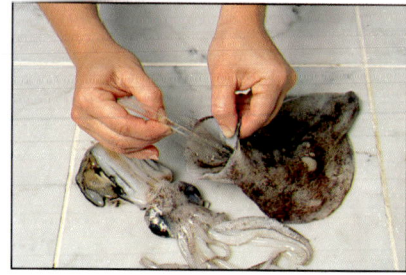

Cut tentacles from head just below eyes; discard head.
Remove side flaps and skin from squid hood with salted fingers. Pull firmly. Wash hood, tentacles and flaps thoroughly.
Cut hood into rings, or use whole. Cut tentacles into pieces and flaps into strips.

REMOVING MEAT FROM CRAB
Hold crab firmly with hand. Slide sharp, strong knife under top of shell at back, lever off shell.

Remove and discard white gills of crab. Cut crabs through centre.

Remove meat from shells with fingers.

Use meat mallet or nut cracker to break claws. Remove meat from claws.

YABBIES, MARRON, SCAMPI
These are prepared the same as a lobster and each can be substituted for the other.

YOUR GUIDE TO SEAFOOD

Whether you buy seafood or catch it yourself, you will find this chart brimming with handy information; we have listed varieties available in Australian and New Zealand waters

FISH

SPECIES	SEASONAL AVAILABILITY	ROUND OR FLAT FISH	THICK OR THIN FILLET	MILD OR FISHY TASTE (STRONGER)	PURCHASING AND EATING QUALITIES	FRY	BAKE	POACH/STEAM	GRILL/BARBECUE	MICROWAVE
ANCHOVY	All year	Round	N/A	Fishy	Small fish, 6cm. Usually eaten whole.	★	★	★	★	★
BARRAMUNDI	Oct-March	Round	Thick	Mild	Available whole (usually frozen) or as fillets. White moist flesh, large flake. Excellent eating.	★	★	★	★	★
BLACKFISH	All year	Round	Thin	Fishy	Usually purchased whole. Soft moist flesh. Pale grey in colour	★	★		★	★
BLUE GRENADIER	Winter	Round	Thick	Mild-fishy	Fillets/cutlets. Pale pink, moist soft flesh; few bones.	★	★	★	★	★
BOAR FISH	All year	Round	Thick	Mild	Whole/fillets. White moist firm flesh, sweet flavour. Excellent eating	★	★	★	★	★
BREAM Sea (morwong)	All year, mainly autumn	Round	Thin	Mild	Whole/fillets. Pale pink, moist, firm flesh.	★	★	★	★	
Silver	All year, mainly March-May	Round	Thin	Mild	Whole. White moist, soft flesh; sweet flavour.	★	★	★	★	★
COD Bar	Winter	Round	Thick	Mild	Fillets/cutlets. White, moist, soft flesh; few bones.	★	★	★	★	★
Blue-eyed	Winter	Round	Thick	Mild	Fillets/cutlets. Soft flesh, mild flavour; few bones	★	★	★	★	★
Red rock	Winter	Round	N/A	Mild	Whole small fish. White, moist, firm flesh. Often called poor man's lobster.	★	★	★		★
CORAL TROUT	All year, mainly winter	Round	Thin	Mild	Whole/fillets. White moist, firm flesh. Excellent eating.	★	★	★	★	★
DARTFISH	Summer-winter	Round	Thick	Mild	Whole/fillets Firm, dryish flesh.	★	★	★		★

SPECIES	SEASONAL AVAILABILITY	ROUND OR FLAT FISH	THICK OR THIN FILLET	MILD OR FISHY TASTE (STRONGER)	PURCHASING AND EATING QUALITIES	FRY	BAKE	POACH/STEAM	GRILL/BARBECUE	MICROWAVE
DORY: John	All year	Round	Thin	Mild	Whole/fillets. White, moist, fine flesh; delicate sweet flavour. No bones in fillets. Excellent eating.	★	★	★	★	★
Mirror or silver	Winter-spring	Round	Thin	Mild	Fillets. White, moist, firm flesh; few bones. Purchase with silver skin intact.	★	★	★	★	★
King	All year, mainly summer	Round	Thin	Mild	Large fillet. White firm flesh.	★	★	★	★	★
EEL	All year	Round	Thick	Fishy	Whole/cutlets. Usually smoked. Pink, soft flesh; fatty flavour.	★	★		★	
EMPEROR (RED)	All year	Round	Thick	Mild	Whole/fillets. White, firm flesh. Excellent eating.	★	★	★	★	★
FLATHEAD	All year, mainly autumn	Round	Thick	Mild	Whole/fillets. White, firm flesh; slightly dry.	★	★	★		★
FLOUNDER	All year	Flat	Thin	Mild	Whole. White, firm flesh; delicate flavour.	★	★	★	★	★
FRESHWATER FISH Perch	All year, mainly spring-autumn.	Round	Thick	Mild	Whole. White, moist flesh; delicate flavour.	★	★	★	★	★
Carp	Late summer	Round	Thick	Fishy	Poor table fish. Can be "muddy" in taste. Slightly dry and bony.	★	★			★
Murray Cod	Mainly July-August	Round	Thick	Mild	Whole. White, moist flesh; delicate flavour.	★	★	★	★	★
Trout	All year	Round	Thin	Mild	Whole. Fresh and smoked. Pink, soft flesh.	★	★	★	★	★
GARFISH	All year	Round	Thin	Mild	Whole. White, firm flesh; sweet flavour, slightly bony.	★	★	★	★	★
GEMFISH	Winter	Round	Thick	Mild-fishy	Fillets/cutlets. (Available frozen all year.) Pinkish, firm, moist flesh. Few bones.	★	★	★	★	★
GOATFISH (Red mullet)	All year	Round	Thin	Mild	Whole. White, soft flesh	★	★	★	★	★
GURNARD (Latchet)	All year	Round	Thick	Mild	Whole/fillets. White, firm flesh; slightly dry.	★	★	★		★
HAIRTAIL	Autumn-winter	Round	Thin	Fishy	Fillets/cutlets. White, soft flesh.	★	★	★	★	★
HERRING	All year	Round	Thin	Fishy	Whole. White, soft flesh; distinct flavour. Slightly oily.	★	★		★	★
JEWFISH	All year, mainly late spring	Round	Thick	Mild	Whole/cutlets. Pinkish, firm, slightly dry flesh.	★	★	★	★	★
JOBFISH	All year	Round	Thick	Mild	Whole/cutlet. Pale pink, firm, moist flesh.	★	★	★	★	★

SPECIES	SEASONAL AVAILABILITY	ROUND OR FLAT FISH	THICK OR THIN FILLET	MILD OR FISHY TASTE (STRONGER)	PURCHASING AND EATING QUALITIES	FRY	BAKE	POACH/STEAM	GRILL/BARBECUE	MICROWAVE
KINGFISH	All year, mainly autumn	Round	Thick	Mild	Whole/fillets/cutlets. Reddish, soft flesh; slightly dry.	★	★	★	★	★
LEATHER-JACKET	All year	Round	Thin	Mild	Whole/skinned. White, firm flesh, few bones.	★	★	★	★	★
LING	Winter	Round	Thick	Mild	Fillets. White, moist fillets; few bones.	★	★	★	★	★
MACKEREL Spanish	Winter	Round	Thick	Fishy	Cutlets. White, soft flesh, slightly dry.	★	★	★		★
Slimmy		Round	Thin	Fishy	Whole smaller fish. Reddish soft flesh, slightly oily.		★	★	★	★
MARLIN	N/A	Round	Thick	Mild	Not available in retail outlets; is caught mostly by leisure fishermen. Firm white flesh.	★	★	★	★	★
MOONFISH	All year	Round	Thick	Mild	Fillets cut from the large whole fish. White, moist flesh; few bones. Excellent eating.	★	★	★	★	★
MULLET	All year, mainly autumn	Round	Thin	Fishy	Whole/fillets. Pinkish soft flesh, slightly oily.		★	★	★	★
OCEAN PERCH	Winter	Round	Thin	Mild	Whole/fillets. Pale pink, firm, delicate flesh. Purchase with red-pink skin intact.	★	★	★	★	★
OCEAN TROUT	All year (farmed fish)	Round	Thick	Mild	Whole/cutlets. Pink, soft flesh; few bones. Excellent eating.	★	★	★	★	★
PARROT	All year, mainly winter	Round	Thick	Mild	Whole. White, soft flesh; delicate flavour.	★	★	★	★	★
PEARL PERCH	Mainly autumn-winter	Round	Thin	Mild	Whole. White, soft flesh; sweet flavour. Excellent eating.	★	★	★	★	★
PIKE	All year	Round	Thin	Mild	Whole small fish. White, soft, sweet, flesh.	★	★	★	★	★
PILCHARDS/SARDINES	All year, mainly winter	Round	Thin	Fishy	Whole small fish. Reddish, soft flesh; slightly oily and bony.	★	★		★	
REDFISH	All year, mainly spring	Round	Thin	Mild	Whole/fillets. Pinkish, firm flesh; slightly bony.	★	★	★	★	★
RIBBONFISH	All year, mainly autumn	Round	Thin	Mild	Whole/cutlets. White, soft flesh.	★	★	★	★	★

SPECIES	SEASONAL AVAILABILITY	ROUND OR FLAT FISH	THICK OR THIN FILLET	MILD OR FISHY TASTE (STRONGER)	PURCHASING AND EATING QUALITIES	FRY	BAKE	POACH/STEAM	GRILL/BARBECUE	MICROWAVE
SALMON Sea	Winter	Round	Thick	Fishy	Whole/cutlets. Firm flesh, slightly dry.	★	★			★
Atlantic (farmed)	All year	Round	Thick	Mild	Whole/cutlets/fillets. Red-pink, firm flesh; moist, delicate flavour; few bones.	★	★	★	★	★
SEA PERCH (Orange roughy)	All year	Round	Thick	Mild	Fillets. White, firm flesh; no bones delicate flavour.	★	★	★	★	★
SHARK (Boneless fillet)	All year	Round	Thick	Mild	Fillets. Pink-white, firm flesh; no bones.	★	★	★	★	★
SILVER BIDDIES	All year	Round	N/A	Mild	Whole small fish. White, soft flesh; slightly bony.	★			★	★
SILVER WAREHOU	Mainly spring	Round	Thick	Fishy	Fillets. White firm flesh; slightly dry.	★	★	★		★
SKATE (Stingray flaps)	All year	N/A	Thick	Mild	White, firm flesh. Sweet flavour; no bones.	★	★	★	★	
SNAPPER	All year, mainly spring	Round	Thin	Mild	Whole/fillets/cutlets. Pink-white, soft flesh; delicate flavour.	★	★	★	★	★
SNOOK	Summer	Round	Thin	Mild	Whole, white soft flesh.	★	★	★	★	
SOLE	All year	Flat	Thin	Mild	Whole/fillets. White, soft flesh; delicate flavour.	★	★	★	★	
SWEEP	All year	Round	Thin	Mild	Whole/fillet. White, soft flesh.	★	★	★	★	★
SWORDFISH	All year	Round	Thick	Mild	Fillets/steaks cut from large fish. White, firm flesh.	★	★	★	★	
TAILOR	Summer	Round	Thin	Fishy	Whole and smoked. Pinkish, soft flesh, slightly oily.	★	★		★	★
TERAGLIN	Spring-summer	Round	Thick	Mild	Whole/fillets. Pink, firm flesh, slightly dry.	★	★	★	★	★
TRUMPETER	Spring-summer	Round	Thick	Mild	Whole/fillets. Pink, moist flesh.	★	★	★	★	★
TREVALLY	All year	Round	Thick	Mild	Whole/fillets. Reddish, firm flesh; slightly dry; no bones.	★	★	★		★
TUNA Bonito, Yellow fin, Blue fin	All year, mainly autumn-winter	Round	Thick	Mild	Fillets, steaks and whole. Reddish, firm flesh; slightly dry; no bones.	★	★	★	★	★
WHITEBAIT (Sprats)	All year	Round	N/A	Fishy	Whole. Small fish eaten whole.	★	★		★	
WHITING	All year	Round	Thin	Mild	Whole/fillets. White firm flesh; delicate sweet flavour.	★	★	★	★	★

SHELLFISH (CRUSTACEANS AND MOLLUSCS)

SPECIES	SEASONAL AVAILABILITY	ROUND OR FLAT FISH	THICK OR THIN FILLET	MILD OR FISHY TASTE (STRONGER)	PURCHASING AND EATING QUALITIES	FRY	BAKE	POACH/STEAM	GRILL/BARBECUE	MICROWAVE
ABALONE	All year	N/A	N/A	Mild	Whole or frozen. White, firm flesh. Requires cooking quickly or long simmer.	★	★	★	★	★
BALMAIN BUGS	All year, mainly summer	N/A	N/A	Mild	Whole, raw or cooked. White firm flesh; sweet, rich flavour.	★	★	★	★	★
COCKLES	All year	N/A	N/A	Fishy	In shell. Reddish, firm flesh; toughen easily.		★	★	★	★

CRABS
  Mud
  Blue Swimmers
  Spanner
	All year, mainly summer	N/A	N/A	Mild	Raw or cooked. White, firm flesh; sweet, delicate flavour.	★	★	★	★	★

CUTTLEFISH	All year	N/A	N/A	Mild	Whole. White, firm flesh; subtle flavour.	★	★	★	★	★

FRESHWATER CRAYFISH
  Yabbies
  Marron
	All year, mainly summer	N/A	N/A	Mild	Alive or cooked. White firm flesh; delicate flavour.	★	★	★	★	★

LOBSTER Crayfish	All year	N/A	N/A	Mild	Alive or cooked. White firm flesh; rich, sweet flavour.	★	★	★	★	★
MUSSELS	All year	N/A	N/A	Fishy	In shell. Yellowish, soft flesh.		★	★	★	★
OCTOPUS	All year	N/A	N/A	Mild	Whole. White, firm flesh; subtle flavour.	★	★	★	★	★
OYSTERS	All year	N/A	N/A	Fishy	In shell or bottle, Greyish, soft texture.	★	★	★	★	★
PIPIS	All year	N/A	N/A	Fishy	In shell. White, firm flesh; toughens easily		★	★	★	★

PRAWNS
  School
  King
  Royal red
	All year	N/A	N/A	Mild	Raw or cooked.	★
						★
							★
							★
								★
								★
									★
									★
										★
										★

Sydney Harbour	Nov-March	N/A	N/A	Mild	Orange-white firm flesh.	★	★	★	★	★
RAZOR CLAMS	All year, but scarce.	N/A	N/A	Fishy	In shell. White, firm flesh.		★	★	★	★
SCALLOPS	All year	N/A	N/A	Fishy	Raw. White-cream soft flesh; delicate flavour. Orange roe is eaten.	★	★	★	★	★
SCAMPI	All year	N/A	N/A	Mild	Raw. White, sweet-flavoured flesh.	★	★	★	★	★

SQUID
  Calamari
  Etheridge
  Arrow or
  Ocean
	All year	N/A	N/A	Mild	Raw, whole or cleaned. White, firm flesh; subtle flavour.	★	★	★	★	★

GLOSSARY

Here are some names, terms and alternatives to help you understand our recipes and use them perfectly.

BACON: rashers are bacon slices
BARBECUE SAUCE: based on tomatoes, sugar and vinegar.
BEEF:
Eye-fillet: tenderloin.
BICARBONATE OF SODA: baking soda.
BOTTLED SPAGHETTI SAUCE: all based on tomatoes, prepared for use over pasta.
BUTTER: we used mostly salted (sweet) butter; a good quality cooking margarine can be used: 1 stick butter = 125g butter.

CHILLI SAUCE: many varieties available, including a sweet variety. Start with less than a teaspoon; add more if required.
CORNFLOUR: cornstarch.
COOKING SALT: a coarse salt.
CRACKED WHEAT: burghul.
CREAM: we have specified thickened (whipping) cream when necessary in recipes; cream is simply a light pouring cream, also known as half 'n' half.
Sour: we used a thick commercially cultured soured cream.

DAIKON: a basic food in Japan, it is also called the giant white radish.

FATHER'S FAVOURITE: spicy sauce based on vinegar, spices and molasses.
FISH SAUCE: made from the liquid drained from salted, fermented anchovies.
FISH STOCK (Basic)
Fish stock can be prepared up to a day ahead; keep, covered, in refrigerator. Stock can be frozen for up to a month. The most convenient way to freeze stock is to reduce it to a smaller amount of liquid. To do this, boil, uncovered, in the saucepan until reduced by half. Cool and freeze in practical portions.
30g butter
2 medium onions, sliced
1kg fish bones and scraps (not eyes)
½ cup dry white wine
4 cups (1 litre) water
6 white peppercorns
6 stems fresh parsley
1 bay leaf
  Melt butter in large saucepan, add onions, stir over medium heat, without browning, for about 5 minutes or until onions are soft. Break fish bones into pieces, wash thoroughly. Add bones to pan with wine and water. Tie remaining ingredients in a piece of muslin, add to stock. Bring stock to boil, reduce heat, simmer, uncovered, for 20 minutes; remove froth from surface of stock as it appears. Strain and cool.
  Makes about 3 cups.
FLOUR:
Plain flour: all-purpose flour.
Self-raising flour: substitute plain (all purpose) flour and baking powder in the proportion of ¾ metric cup plain flour to 2 level metric teaspoons baking powder, sift the mixture together several times before using. If using an 8oz measuring cup, use 1 cup plain flour to 2 level metric teaspoons baking powder.
Wholemeal flour: wholewheat flour; add baking powder as above to make wholemeal self-raising flour.

GHERKIN: cornichon.
GINGER: fresh (green or root) ginger; scrape away skin and it is ready to grate, chop or slice. Preserved/pickled ginger can be sweet or salted.
GREEN SHALLOTS: spring onions/scallions.
GRILL, GRILLER: broil, broiler.

HERBS: we have specified when to use fresh or dried herbs. We used dried (not ground) herbs in the proportion of 1:4 for fresh herbs; for example, 1 teaspoon dried herbs instead of 4 teaspoons (1 tablespoon) chopped fresh herbs.
HOISIN SAUCE: a thick sweet Chinese barbecue sauce made from salted black beans, onions and garlic.

KUMARA: orange-coloured sweet potato.

LAMINGTON PAN: a rectangular slab pan with a depth of about 4cm.
LEMON GRASS: available from Asian food stores and needs to be bruised or chopped before using. It will keep in a jug of water at room temperature for several weeks; the water must be changed daily. It can be bought dried: to reconstitute: place several pieces of dried lemon grass in a bowl, cover with hot water, stand 20 minutes; drain. This amount is a substitute for 1 stem of fresh lemon grass.

MIRIN: a sweet rice wine used in Japanese cooking. Substitute 1 teaspoon sugar and 1 teaspoon dry sherry for each 1 tablespoon mirin.
MUSTARD, SEEDED: a French style of mustard with crushed mustard seeds.

OIL: use a light polyunsaturated salad oil.
OYSTER SAUCE: a thick sauce made from oysters cooked in salt and soy sauce.

PEPPERS: capsicum or bell peppers.
PIMIENTOS: sweet red peppers preserved in brine in cans or jars.
PUNNET: basket holding about 250g fruit.

RICE BUBBLES: rice crispies.
RIND: zest.
ROCKMELON: cantaloupe.

SAMBAL OELEK: a paste made from ground chillies and salt.
SEAFOOD STICKS: made from processed Alaskan pollack flavoured with crab.
SESAME OIL: made from roasted, crushed white sesame seeds. It is always used in small quantities. Do not use for frying.
SOY SAUCE: made from fermented soy beans. The light sauce is generally used with white meat for flavour, and the darker variety with red meat for colour. There is a multi-purpose salt-reduced sauce available, also Japanese soy sauce. It is personal taste which sauce you use.
SNOW PEAS: also known as mange tout, sugar peas or Chinese peas.
SPINACH:
English spinach: a soft-leafed vegetable, more delicate in taste than silverbeet (spinach); however, young silverbeet can be substituted for English spinach.
Silverbeet: a large-leafed vegetable; remove white stalk before cooking.
SPRING ROLL WRAPPERS OR PASTRY: are sold frozen, thaw before using, keep covered with a damp cloth while using.
STOCK CUBES: 1 small stock cube is equivalent to 1 teaspoon powdered bouillon; 1 large stock cube is equivalent to 2 teaspoons powdered bouillon.
SULTANAS: seedless white raisins.
SUN-DRIED TOMATOES: are dried tomatoes sometimes bottled in oil.
SWEET GROUND BEAN SAUCE: a mixture of soy beans, flour, salt, sugar and water. Add 1 teaspoon sugar to 1 tablespoon black bean sauce, if preferred.

TAMARIND SAUCE: made from tamarinds. If unavailable, soak about 30g dried tamarinds in a cup of water, stand 10 minutes. Squeeze the pulp as dry as possible and use the flavoured water.
TERIYAKI MARINADE: a blend of soy sauce, wine, vinegar and spices.
TERIYAKI SAUCE: based on the lighter Japanese soy sauce; contains sugar, spices and vinegar.
TOM YUM: a sweet and sour shrimp paste used mostly in cooking Indonesian recipes.
TOMATO PUREE: known as tomato sauce in some countries.
TOMATO SAUCE: tomato ketchup.

YEAST: 3 level teaspoons dried yeast can be substituted for 30g compressed yeast.
WATER CHESTNUTS: small white crisp bulbs with a brown skin. Canned water chestnuts are peeled and will keep for about a month in the refrigerator.
WONTON WRAPPERS: are thin squares or rounds of fresh noodle dough. They are sold frozen; cover with damp cloth to prevent drying while using.

ZUCCHINI: courgette.

INDEX

Anchovy Dip, Hot	12
Anchovy, Olive and Onion Quiche	58
Anchovy Pizzas, Mini	115
Asparagus Bake, Crunchy-Topped Prawn and	56
Asparagus Salad, Tuna	84
Bagels, Salmon	74
Balmain Bug Cocktails	8
Balmain Bugs in Brandy Cream Sauce	34
Balmain Bugs in Puff Pastry Cases	20
Balmain Bugs with Lime Butter	103
Barbecued Fish with Herb and Bacon Butter	108
Basil Sauce, Lobster Medallions with Macadamia	23
Batter, Fish in Coconut Beer	60
Batter, Seafood in Tempura	90
Beer Batter, Fish in Coconut	60
Beignets, Cheesy Salmon	85
Beurre Blanc, Fish with Passionfruit	32
Bisque, Prawn	5
Black Bean Sauce, Crispy Fish Balls in	46
Butterflied Sardines with Minted Pineapple Sauce	105
Camembert Fish Rolls with Lime Sauce, Prawn and	33
Cannelloni, Fish and Spinach	93
Carpet Bag Steak Sizzlers	109
Casserole, Layered Eggplant and Fish	56
Casseroles, Mini Tuna, Tomato and Pasta	77
Caviar Hollandaise, Poached Salmon with	43
Cheesy Salmon Beignets	85
Chicken and Crab with Avocado Sauce	40
Chicken Pâté, Squid with Nutty	10
Chilli Mud Crabs, Sweet	41
Chilli Seafood Frittata	58
Chunky Fish with Ginger Peppercorn Sauce	29
Clear Baby Octopus Soup	6
Clear Soup with Garfish Twists	4
Cockle and Broccoli Salad	12
Coconut Beer Batter, Fish in	60
Coconut Cream Soup with Spinach and Kumara	4
Coconut Cream Soup, Seafood with	2
Cold Salmon and Egg Pie	74
Coriander Vinaigrette, Ocean Trout with Warm	36
Corn Muffins with Cheese Spread, Salmon and	91
Corn Pancakes with Spicy Yoghurt Salad, Crab and	96
Cottage Pie, Fish	55
Crab and Corn Pancakes with Spicy Yoghurt Salad	96
Crab and Watercress Soup	5
Crab Nachos	95
Crabs, Sweet Chilli Mud	41
Crab Terrine, Ocean Trout and	78
Crab with Avocado Sauce, Chicken and	40
Crackly Fish Strips	111
Cream of Mussel Soup	7
Creamy Fish and Potato Bake	52
Creamy Leek and Oyster Soup	2
Creamy Prawn Puff Cases	85
Creamy Salmon Sauce with Pasta	63
Creamy Salmon with Mushrooms	58
Crêpe Cornets, Prawn and Mushroom	24
Crêpe Rollups, Salmon	24
Crêpe Stack, Tuna	114
Crêpes with Creamy Fish Filling, Wholemeal	58
Crispy Fish Balls in Black Bean Sauce	46
Croquettes, Smoked Fish	92
Croustade, Quick Fish	77
Crumbed Fish with Tomato Onion Sauce	50
Crumbed Squid with Tomato Sauce	95
Crunchy-Coated Fish Loaf	80
Crunchy Potato-Topped Tuna Bake	52
Crunchy-Topped Prawn and Asparagus Bake	56
Crunchy-Topped Smoked Fish with Broccoli	54
Crusty Baked Fish Cutlets	60
Crusty Baked Smoked Salmon Puff	72
Crusty-Topped Salmon Bake	78
Curried Prawn and Vegetable Stir-Fry	46
Curried Prawns and Vegetables	48
Curried Smoked Fish and Pea Soup	4
Curried Smoked Fish Pasties	48
Cuttlefish with Fettucine and Pesto	26
Cuttlefish with Tamarind Lemon Grass Sauce	10
Deep-Fried Prawns with Seasoned Salt	82
Eel and Leek Quiche, Smoked	86
Eel Pâté, Smoked	10
Eggplant and Fish Casserole, Layered	56
Fish and Bacon Pie	92
Fish and Bean Hot Pot, Hearty	56
Fish and Carrot Rolls with Mint Coriander Sauce	71
Fish and Macaroni Pie	66
Fish and Mushrooms in Lettuce Cups, Stir-Fried	112
Fish and Pepper Satays	19
Fish and Potato Bake, Creamy	52
Fish and Potato Loaf with Fresh Tomato Sauce	47
Fish and Potato Scallops with Tartare Sauce	68
Fish and Rice Puff	45
Fish and Spaghetti Frittata	73
Fish and Spinach Cannelloni	93
Fish and Spinach Lasagne	87
Fish and Vegetable Hot Pot	55
Fish and Vegetable Pasties	111
Fish and Vegetable Pie, Smoked	68
Fish and Vegetable Puffs, Oriental	89
Fish Balls in Black Bean Sauce, Crispy	46
Fish Balls with Spaghetti, Saucy	114
Fish Burgers	102
Fish Cakes with Cucumber and Mint Chutney	101
Fish Casserole, Layered Eggplant and	56
Fish Cottage Pie	55
Fish Croquettes, Smoked	92
Fish Croustade, Quick	77
Fish Cutlets, Crusty Baked	60
Fish Cutlets, Green Peppercorn and Lemon	101
Fish Cutlets, Olive Seasoned	109
Fish Cutlets with Chilli Bean Sauce, Hearty	64
Fish Cutlets with Creamy Corn Sauce, Pan-Fried	60
Fish Cutlets with Hazelnut Hollandaise	38
Fish Cutlets with Spinach Hollandaise	35
Fish Fillets with Chervil Cream Sauce	33
Fish Finger Toasties, Lemon	96
Fish Florentine	48
Fish in Coconut Beer Batter	60
Fish Loaf, Crunchy-Coated	80
Fish Meuniére	62
Fish, Minted Apricot	48
Fish Parcels with Lemon Sauce	105
Fish Pasties, Curried Smoked	48
Fish Patties with Lemon and Chive Mayonnaise	47
Fish Paupiettes with Lemon Pepper Sauce	15
Fish, Pepper and Potato Kebabs	83
Fish Ring, Smoked	51
Fish Rolls with Lime Sauce, Prawn and Camembert	33
Fish Rolls with Sweet and Sour Sauce	113
Fish Roll with Chunky Tomato Sauce, Herbed	80
Fish Roulade, Pumpkin and	85
Fish Sandwiches	111
Fish Sausages, Tasty	112
Fish Strips, Crackly	111
Fish, Tasty Herbed Crumbed	64
Fish Wellington with Mushroom Sauce	36
Fish with Bacon and Mushroom Sauce, Pan-Fried	57
Fish with Broccoli, Crunchy-Topped Smoked	54
Fish with Citrus Sauce, Poached	29
Fish with Fresh Herb Butter, Grilled	96
Fish with Ginger Peppercorn Sauce, Chunky	29
Fish with Ginger Sauce, Steamed Whole	35
Fish with Herb and Bacon Butter, Barbecued	108
Fish with Lemon Soufflé Topping and Pimiento Coulis	38
Fish with Lime Butter Sauce, Peppered	30
Fish with Mustard Glaze, Whole	52
Fish with Passionfruit Beurre Blanc	32
Fish with Spicy Seasoning	102
Fish with Sweet and Sour Sauce, Pan-Fried	68
Fish with Tomato Onion Sauce, Crumbed	50
Fish with Vegetable Seasoning, Whole	66
Fishyssoise Soup	7
Fried Rice, Seafood	54
Frittata, Chilli Seafood	58
Frittata, Fish and Spaghetti	73
Frittata, Tuna and Kumara	113
Fritters, Prawn and Rice	98
Fritters with Lemon Mustard Mayonnaise, Oyster	16
Garfish Rolls, Skewered	102
Garfish Twists, Clear Soup with	4
Garlic Prawns, Peppered	27
Gnocchi with Seafood Sauce	98
Gravlax	27
Green Peppercorn and Lemon Fish Cutlets	101
Grilled Fish with Fresh Herb Butter	96
Hearty Fish and Bean Hot Pot	56
Hearty Fish Cutlets with Chilli Bean Sauce	64
Herbed Fish Roll with Chunky Tomato Sauce	80
Honeyed Prawns, Skewered	109
Honey Lime Lobster with Avocado Cream	30
Hot Anchovy Dip	12
Kebabs, Fish, Pepper and Potato	83
Kebabs, Marinated Squid and Water Chestnut	104
Kokoda	89
Lamb Rolls with Smoked Salmon	40
Lasagne, Fish and Spinach	87
Layered Eggplant and Fish Casserole	56
Leek and Oyster Soup, Creamy	2
Lemon Fish Finger Toasties	96
Lemon Grass Sauce, Cuttlefish with Tamarind	10
Lobster Medallions with Creamy Peppercorn Sauce	23
Lobster Medallions with Macadamia Basil Sauce	23
Lobster Tails with Orange Pine Nut Butter	106
Lobster Thermidor with Crunchy Topping	35
Lobster with Avocado Cream, Honey Lime	30
Mango and Macadamia Salad, Prawn,	83
Marinated Squid and Water Chestnut Kebabs	104
Meuniére, Fish	62
Mini Anchovy Pizzas	115
Mini Steamed Buns with Seafood Sauce	90
Minted Apricot Fish	48

Mousseline, Sole with Herb and Prawn	34
Mud Crabs, Sweet Chilli	41
Muffins with Cheese Spread, Salmon and Corn	91
Mushroom Crêpe Cornets, Prawn and	24
Mussels and Pine Nuts, Pasta with	87
Mussel Soup, Cream of	7
Mussels with Spicy Honey Glaze, Skewered	101
Mussels with Two Toppings	22
Nachos, Crab	95
Ocean Trout and Crab Terrine	78
Ocean Trout with Warm Coriander Vinaigrette	36
Octopus Soup, Clear Baby	6
Octopus with Cucumber Vinaigrette, Pickled	14
Octopus with Pine Nuts, Sultanas and Basil	106
Olive Seasoned Fish Cutlets	109
Omelette, Prawn and Mushroom	82
Onion Quiche, Anchovy, Olive and	58
Open Sandwiches	78
Oriental Fish and Vegetable Puffs	89
Oyster and Bacon Parcels	32
Oyster Fritters with Lemon Mustard Mayonnaise	16
Pancakes with Spicy Yoghurt Salad, Crab and Corn	96
Pan-Fried Fish Cutlets with Creamy Corn Sauce	60
Pan-Fried Fish with Bacon and Mushroom Sauce	57
Pan-Fried Fish with Sweet and Sour Sauce	68
Pan-Fried Snapper Tails with Creamed Peppers	29
Pasta with Mussels and Pine Nuts	87
Pasties, Curried Smoked Fish	48
Pasties, Fish and Vegetable	111
Pâté, Smoked Eel	10
Pâté, Squid with Nutty Chicken	10
Patties with Lemon and Chive Mayonnaise, Fish	47
Paupiettes with Blue Cheese Sauce, Pork and Prawn	43
Paupiettes with Lemon Pepper Sauce, Fish	15
Peppered Fish with Lime Butter Sauce	30
Peppered Garlic Prawns	27
Pesto, Cuttlefish with Fettucine and	26
Pickled Octopus with Cucumber Vinaigrette	14
Pie, Cold Salmon and Egg	74
Pie, Fish and Bacon	92
Pie, Fish and Macaroni	66
Pie, Fish Cottage	55
Pie, Smoked Fish and Vegetable	68
Pilaf, Tuna and Cashew	62
Pipis with Orange Herb Butter	21
Pizza, Seafood and Bacon	44
Pizzas, Mini Anchovy	115
Poached Fish with Citrus Sauce	29
Poached Salmon with Caviar Hollandaise	43
Pork and Prawn Paupiettes with Blue Cheese Sauce	43
Potato and Salmon Salad	93
Potato Loaf with Fresh Tomato Sauce, Fish and	47
Potato Scallops with Tartare Sauce, Fish and	68
Potato-Topped Tuna Bake, Crunchy	52
Prawn and Asparagus Bake, Crunchy-Topped	56
Prawn and Camembert Fish Rolls with Lime Sauce	33
Prawn and Mushroom Crêpe Cornets	24
Prawn and Mushroom Omelette	82
Prawn and Rice Fritters	98
Prawn and Vegetable Stir-Fry, Curried	46
Prawn Bisque	5
Prawn, Mango and Macadamia Salad	83
Prawn Mousseline, Sole with Herb and	34
Prawn Paupiettes with Blue Cheese Sauce, Pork and	43
Prawn Puff Cases, Creamy	85
Prawn Quenelles, Scallop and	23
Prawns and Vegetables, Curried	48
Prawns in Herbed Tomato Sauce with Feta Cheese	26
Prawns, Peppered Garlic	27
Prawns, Skewered Honeyed	109
Prawns with Apricot and Pine Nut Seasoning	27
Prawns with Garlic and Currants	29
Prawns with Seasoned Salt, Deep-Fried	82
Prawn Toasted Sandwiches, Tasty	73
Prawn Wonton Soup	6
Pumpkin and Fish Roulade	85
Pumpkin with Prawns in Coconut Cream Sauce	86
Quenelles, Scallop and Prawn	23
Quiche, Anchovy, Olive and Onion	58
Quiche, Smoked Eel and Leek	86
Quick Fish Croustade	77
Ravioli with Vermouth, Seafood	18
Roulade, Pumpkin and Fish	85
Salad, Cockle and Broccoli	12
Salad, Crab and Corn Pancakes with Spicy Yoghurt	96
Salad in Pita Pockets, Smoked Trout	89
Salad, Potato and Salmon	93
Salad, Prawn, Mango and Macadamia	83
Salad, Squid and Tomato	14
Salad, Tuna Asparagus	84
Salad with Avocado Dressing, Seafood	12
Salmon and Corn Muffins with Cheese Spread	91
Salmon and Cream Cheese Rollups	74
Salmon and Egg Pie, Cold	74
Salmon and Vegetable Sauce with Pasta	66
Salmon Bagels	74
Salmon Bake, Crusty-Topped	78
Salmon Beignets, Cheesy	85
Salmon Crêpe Rollups	24
Salmon Cutlets with Fresh Herb Sauce	30
Salmon Dip, Seafood Platter with Warm	39
Salmon Feta Rolls, Spinach and	85
Salmon, Lamb Rolls with Smoked	40
Salmon Mould, Cucumber and	80
Salmon Pithiviers with Pepper Bearnaise	18
Salmon Puff, Crusty Baked Smoked	72
Salmon Salad, Potato and	93
Salmon Sauce with Pasta, Creamy	63
Salmon with Caviar Hollandaise, Poached	43
Salmon with Mushrooms, Creamy	58
Salmon with Sour Cream-Stuffed Potatoes	105
Sardine Finger Sandwiches	113
Sardines with Basil and Olive Seasoning	25
Sardines with Minted Pineapple Sauce, Butterflied	105
Sashimi with Orange Ginger Dressing	16
Satays, Fish and Pepper	19
Saucy Fish Balls with Spaghetti	114
Scallop and Prawn Quenelles	23
Scallops with Chineses Vegetables	90
Scallops with Tartare Sauce, Fish and Potato	68
Scampi with Champagne Sauce	42
Seafood and Bacon Pizza	44
Seafood and Pasta Italiana	95
Seafood Curry Sauce with Pasta	63
Seafood Fried Rice	54
Seafood Frittatta, Chilli	58
Seafood in Crisp Pastry Parcels	20
Seafood in Rich Tomato Sauce	65
Seafood in Tempura Batter	90
Seafood Platter with Warm Salmon Dip	39
Seafood Ravioli with Vermouth	18
Seafood Salad with Avocado Dressing	12
Seafood Spinach Terrine	8
Seafood Vegetable Spring Rolls	89
Seafood with Coconut Cream Soup	2
Sesame Seed Whitebait	25
Skewered Garfish Rolls	102
Skewered Honeyed Prawns	109
Skewered Mussels with Spicy Honey Glaze	101
Smoked Eel and Leek Quiche	86
Smoked Eel Pâté	10
Smoked Fish and Pea Soup, Curried	4
Smoked Fish and Saffron Rice Slice	74
Smoked Fish and Vegetable Cake	76
Smoked Fish and Vegetable Pie	68
Smoked Fish Croquettes	92
Smoked Fish Pasties, Curried	48
Smoked Fish Ring	51
Smoked Fish with Broccoli, Crunchy-Topped	54
Smoked Salmon, Lamb Rolls with	40
Smoked Salmon Puff, Crusty Baked	72
Smoked Trout Salad in Pita Pockets	89
Smoked Trout Timbales with Red Pepper Sauce	15
Snapper Tails with Creamed Peppers, Pan-Fried	29
Snapper with Shallots and Red Pepper Seasoning	108
Sole with Herb and Prawn Mousseline	34
Soufflé, Trout	91
Spaghetti Frittata, Fish and	73
Spaghetti, Saucy Fish Balls with	114
Spinach and Salmon Feta Rolls	85
Spinach Bake, Tuna and	50
Spinach Cannelloni, Fish and	93
Spinach Lasagne, Fish and	87
Spinach Terrine, Seafood	8
Spring Rolls, Seafood Vegetable	89
Squid and Tomato Salad	14
Squid and Water Chestnut Kebabs, Marinated	104
Squid in Mustard Cream	10
Squid with Chutney, Honey and Garlic	106
Squid with Nutty Chicken Pâté	10
Squid with Tomato Sauce, Crumbed	95
Steak Sizzlers, Carpet Bag	109
Steamed Buns with Seafood Sauce, Mini	90
Steamed Whole Fish with Ginger Sauce	35
Stir-Fried Fish and Mushrooms in Lettuce Cups	112
Stir-Fry, Curried Prawn and Vegetable	46
Stir-Fry, Sweet Bug Tail	70
Sweet and Sour Sauce, Fish Rolls with	113
Sweet and Sour Sauce, Pan-Fried Fish with	68
Sweet Bug Tail Stir-Fry	70
Sweet Chilli Mud Crabs	41
Tartare Sauce, Fish and Potato Scallops with	68
Tasty Fish Sausages	112
Tasty Herbed Crumbed Fish	64
Tasty Prawn Toasted Sandwiches	73
Tempura Batter, Seafood in	90
Terrine, Ocean Trout and Crab	78
Terrine, Seafood Spinach	8
Themidor with Crunchy Topping, Lobster	35
Timbales with Red Pepper Sauce, Smoked Trout	15
Tomato and Pasta Casseroles, Mini Tuna,	77
Tomato Soup with Chunky Seafood	6
Torpodoes with Creamy Tomato Sauce	115
Trout and Crab Terrine, Ocean	78
Trout Salad in Pita Pockets, Smoked	89
Trout Soufflé	91
Trout Timbales with Red Pepper Sauce, Smoked	15
Trout with Warm Coriander Vinaigrette, Ocean	36
Tuna and Cashew Pilaf	62
Tuna and Corn Plait	76
Tuna and Kumara Frittata	113
Tuna and Sesame Snacks	98
Tuna and Spinach Bake	50
Tuna Asparagus Salad	84
Tuna Bake, Crunchy Potato-Topped	52
Tuna Crêpe Stack	114
Tuna, Tomato and Pasta Casseroles, Mini	77
Watercress Soup, Crab and	5
Whitebait, Sesame Seed	25
Whole Fish with Ginger Sauce, Steamed	35
Whole Fish with Mustard Glaze	52
Whole Fish with Vegetable Seasoning	66
Wholemeal Crêpes with Creamy Fish Filling	58